After Jesus was born in Bethlehem in Judea, during the time of King Herod, Magi from the east came to Jerusalem and asked, "Where is the one who has been born king of the Jews? We saw his star when it rose and have come to worship him."

When King Herod heard this he was disturbed, and all Jerusalem with him. When he had called together all the people's chief priests and teachers of the law, he asked them where the Messiah was to be born. "In Bethlehem in Judea," they replied, "for this is what the prophet has written:

"'But you, Bethlehem, in the land of Judah,
are by no means least among the rulers of Judah;
for out of you will come a ruler
who will shepherd my people Israel.'"

Then Herod called the Magi secretly and found out from them the exact time the star had appeared. He sent them to Bethlehem and said, "Go and search carefully for the child. As soon as you find him, report to me, so that I too may go and worship him."

After they had heard the king, they went on their way, and the star they had seen when it rose went ahead of them until it stopped over the place where the child was. When they saw the star, they were overjoyed. On coming to the house, they saw the child with his mother Mary, and they bowed down and worshiped him. Then they opened their treasures and presented him with gifts of gold, frankincense and myrrh. And having been warned in a dream not to go back to Herod, they returned to their country by another route.

—Matthew 2:1–12 (NIV)

Mysteries & Wonders of the Bible

Unveiled: Tamar's Story
A Life Renewed: Shoshan's Story
Garden of Secrets: Adah's Story
Among the Giants: Achsah's Story
Seeking Leviathan: Milkah's Story
A Flame of Hope: Abital's Story
Covenant of the Heart: Odelia's Story
Treacherous Waters: Zahla's Story
Star of Wonder: Dobah's Story

MYSTERIES & WONDERS of the BIBLE

STAR OF WONDER
DOBAH'S STORY

Robin Lee Hatcher

Guideposts

A Gift from Guideposts

Thank you for your purchase! We want to express our gratitude for your support with a special gift just for you.

Dive into **Spirit Lifters**, a complimentary e-book that will fortify your faith, offering solace during challenging moments. Its 31 carefully selected scripture verses will soothe and uplift your soul.

Please use the QR code or go to **guideposts.org/spiritlifters** to download.

Mysteries & Wonders of the Bible is a trademark of Guideposts.

Published by Guideposts
100 Reserve Road, Suite E200, Danbury, CT 06810
Guideposts.org

Copyright © 2025 by Guideposts. All rights reserved. This book, or parts thereof, may not be reproduced, stored in a retrieval system, or transmitted in any form or by any means, electronic, mechanical, photocopying, recording, or otherwise, without the written permission of the publisher.

This is a work of fiction. While the characters and settings are drawn from scripture references and historical accounts, apart from the actual people, events, and locales that figure into the fiction narrative, all other names, characters, places, and events are the creation of the author's imagination or are used fictitiously. Every attempt has been made to credit the sources of copyrighted material used in this book. If any such acknowledgment has been inadvertently omitted or miscredited, receipt of such information would be appreciated.

Scripture references are from the following sources: *The Holy Bible, King James Version* (KJV). *The Holy Bible, New International Version* (NIV). Copyright © 1973, 1978, 1984, 2011 by Biblica, Inc. Used by permission of Zondervan. All rights reserved worldwide. www.zondervan.com.

Cover and interior design by Müllerhaus
Cover illustration by Brian Call represented by Illustration Online LLC.
Typeset by Aptara, Inc.

ISBN 978-1-961441-90-3 (hardcover)
ISBN 978-1-961441-91-0 (softcover)
ISBN 978-1-961441-92-7 (epub)

Printed and bound in the United States of America
10 9 8 7 6 5 4 3 2 1

MYSTERIES & WONDERS of the BIBLE

STAR OF WONDER
DOBAH'S STORY

CAST OF CHARACTERS

Boaz ben David • father of Dobah, tribe of Judah, brother of Yosef's mother Gila

Dobah • cousin of Yosef, widow, mother of Levi

Ethan • Menes's new name after his conversion

Keziah • Machla's sister, aunt to Dobah, Bethsaida

Levi • Dobah's oldest son

Machla • mother of Dobah, wife of Boaz

Menes • a khabir for the magi, an Egyptian (see Ethan)

Miryam • wife of Yosef/Joseph

Yeshua • a son of Yosef and Miryam, the Messiah

Yosef ben Yakov • cousin of Dobah, husband of Miryam/Mary

GLOSSARY OF TERMS

abba • father

agora • public market and gathering area

Beth Sefer • synagogue school for boys and girls, ages five to ten, focusing on the Written Torah & memorization skills

Beth Talmud • synagogue school for boys only, ages ten to thirteen, engaging and memorizing the rest of Scripture (Tanakh) and beginning to learn the Oral Torah

chuppah • a Jewish wedding canopy (sometimes spelled huppah)

decuria • a Roman cavalry unit made up of ten men

decurion • the commander of a decuria

ger • sojourner

ger tzedek • righteous convert

Hallel • a prayer of thanksgiving added to the morning service on festive Jewish holidays

imma • mother

kataluma • guest room (translated "inn" in some English versions of the Bible); also spelled katalyma

khabir • someone with expertise and knowledge; in this book, the expert leader of a caravan

Ketuvim • "The Writings," the third and final division of the Tanakh

mezuzah • a small case affixed to the doorframe, which contains a tiny scroll of parchment inscribed with a prayer

mikveh • a ritual bath

naggara • Hebrew for artisan/craftsman (similar to the Greek tekton, often translated as carpenter in English Bibles)

Nevi'im • "The Prophets," the second major division of the Hebrew Bible

Pesach • Passover

Ruach HaKodesh • the Holy Spirit

saba • grandfather (Aramaic)

savta • grandmother (Aramaic)

sukkah • a booth or hut (the plural in Hebrew is sukkot) in which Jews are supposed to dwell during the weeklong celebration of Sukkot

talmid • a disciple who seeks to become exactly like their master; plural is talmidim

Tanakh • the Jewish Bible, called the Old Testament by Christians

tekton • a common term for an artisan/craftsman, in particular a carpenter, woodworker, stoneworker, or builder

Torah • first five books of the Old Testament

CHAPTER ONE

In the month of Tevet, 5 BC

Dobah held Levi's hand as he took two steps toward his favorite toy, his happy babble bouncing off the walls of the small room attached to her abba's house, the room she shared with her eleven-month-old son as well as her *savta*. Her savta instead of her husband.

Tears welled, but she blinked them away. It did not serve to wish for what could never be. Dover, her husband, had been dead for more than a year. She could not bring him back, no matter how much she wished she could. She could not change what had happened to him, the accident that had taken his life and left her a young pregnant widow, forced to return home to live with her parents once again.

The sound of *Imma*'s singing in the small courtyard drifted to her, and she lifted Levi into her arms before leaving the room and walking to the front door.

The census commanded by Rome had swelled Bethlehem's population to at least twice its normal size. But now, at last, people had started to return to their own homes. The guest room of Boaz ben David's house had been filled to capacity with male family members who had traveled to the village in obedience to the decree. A few had even slept in the stable. But today, the last of their relations had departed.

"Yosef!"

Dobah heard her imma's cry of delight and saw her arms reach out in a gesture of welcome. Yosef, Dobah's favorite cousin! She darted out into the small courtyard.

There he was, beyond the stone fence, her impossibly handsome cousin. Yosef ben Yakov. And with him was his wife, Miryam, their baby—a few days old now—in her arms.

"Are you ready for us, Machla?" Yosef asked Dobah's imma.

"The *kataluma* is empty at last," Imma answered. "Come in. You can wash your feet and have something to eat and drink."

Balancing Levi on her hip, Dobah moved to open the gate for them.

"Hello, Cousin," Yosef said to her, smiling. His gaze shifted to her son. "Is this Levi? Look how he has grown."

"Yes." She rose on tiptoe and kissed Yosef's cheek. "It is good to see you again."

"And you? How are you?" He gave his head the slightest shake. "I am sorry about Dover. I know it is still hard."

A lump rose in her throat, and she nodded in answer.

Yosef reached back and drew Miryam to his side. "Dobah, this is my wife, Miryam. Miryam, this is my cousin Dobah and her son, Levi."

Miryam's smile was shy. "Yosef has told me much of his family in Bethlehem."

"All good, I hope."

Yosef laughed. "All true, at least."

Imma stepped closer. "We are so sorry there was no room for you until now." Her gaze flicked to the baby. "It is not what we would have wanted. You should not have had to be alone at such a time."

"Adonai provided," Yosef responded softly.

"Come in. You are with family at last." Imma led the way into the house, Yosef and Miryam right behind her. Dobah waited a few moments by the gate, allowing memories to wash over her. Sweet memories of family gatherings—for weddings, births, festivals, and more. So much love. She was blessed to be part of such a family. None of them were wealthy, but money could not buy what was most important.

Levi pumped his arms and squealed his demand for action. Smiling again, she hurried toward the doorway of their home.

The main floor of the Boaz ben David home had one large room for living, eating, and cooking, plus a sleeping area beneath the kataluma. The doorway to Dobah and Savta's room was also at the back, while a narrow staircase against the wall led to the kataluma. To the left of the main entrance and down three steps was the small stable where the family's livestock—two goats and a donkey—stayed during the night.

"It is such a long way from Nazareth," Imma was saying when Dobah entered the house. "And then to be forced to stay with strangers without a room to yourself. To give birth without loved ones around you."

"Do not concern yourself, Machla." Yosef put a hand on Miryam's shoulder. "We are well."

"Such a difficult time." Imma tsked softly. "It is cruel, what the Romans have done. Your wife should not have had to travel so far at such a time."

"My place was with my husband." The look Miryam gave Yosef was shy and a little uncertain.

Dobah remembered feeling that way with Dover when they were first betrothed. Even after their marriage had been consummated, she'd been unsure what to say or do so much of the time. But at least, when it had come time for her to give birth, she'd been with Imma and her two married sisters. Miryam, on the other hand, had been far from family and friends.

"Your uncle Boaz will return from the vineyard soon," Imma said, pulling Dobah from her thoughts. "He will be glad to see you."

Dobah set Levi on the floor and went to check the stew that simmered above the cook fire. Fresh bread waited on a nearby table, along with cheese, olive oil, and wine. While Bethlehem burst at the seams because of the census, it had been difficult to find items to buy in the market. Her *abba* was more prosperous than many of their neighbors, but even he could not purchase what was not available. Dobah hoped the situation would improve as life returned to normal, especially now that Yosef and Miryam would be with them until baby Yeshua's dedication.

Male laughter from the street announced the return of Boaz from the vineyard. Yosef stood mere seconds before the door opened. But it wasn't her abba who came through the opening first. It was her savta, a tiny woman with deeply wrinkled skin and a near-toothless smile.

"Savta!" Yosef moved to embrace the grandmother he shared with Dobah, lifting her feet off the floor and knocking the scarf from her gray head.

"Put me down," the old woman demanded with a laugh.

He obeyed.

Boaz entered then, and the two men exchanged hugs and slaps on the back.

Dobah smiled as she watched them. It was good they could all be together. Abba would enjoy having Yosef with him during the day at the vineyard, and Imma would love having another infant to fuss over. And young Miryam would have nearly six weeks to rest until the temple dedication. Then she would be ready for Yosef to take her and the baby on the long journey north to Nazareth.

Camels complained, as usual, as the caravan set off on its nightly journey. The sounds were familiar to Menes. As familiar to him as the sound of his own voice, for he had heard the animals' grunts and hums for most of his twenty-five years.

Menes could scarcely remember when he hadn't traveled great distances with caravans, both large and small. Caravans that had taken him from Egypt to Arabia to Syria to Asia. Again and again and then again. He had been a boy of no more than seven when he'd set out on his first journey, apprenticed to a khabir, a man of great knowledge and experience. Now a khabir himself and the owner of many camels, Menes hoped this would be his final trip for a while.

His gaze went to the bright light in the sky, and a shiver of anticipation went through him. In all his years, he had never seen anything like it, nor had he been on a journey quite like this one. The magi who had hired him in a city near the Tigris River had told him the light would guide them to their destination. If they were such wise men, as others purported, how could they set off without knowing where they wanted to end up? It seemed a fool's errand. However, they had paid him well. Who was he to say they should know better?

His body rolling with the gait of the camel, he looked behind him. The prosperity of the magi was not in question. Their robes were of the finest quality, and the camels that followed them were laden with precious oils and gold. He had seen their wealth for himself, which was why he also had seen to the hiring of numerous guards to protect them.

He looked ahead, his gaze lifting a second time to the star. It was a wonder. Nearly as bright as a full moon and different from other stars. It didn't remain in the same place night after night. It moved ahead of them. The magi said it would lead them to meet a new king. Menes had doubted the truth of it at first, but the star did seem to be leading them.

Perhaps they were wise men after all.

CHAPTER TWO

In the month of Shevat, 4 BC

While the family waited for the forty days of Miryam's purification to be completed, as required in the law of Moshe, life in Bethlehem returned to normal. The people who had come from far away for the Roman census were gone, and the village streets were quiet most of the time. Thus, Dobah's days were much the same as the ones that had passed before. Yosef went to work with Dobah's abba in the vineyard and—being a *tekton* who loved to work with his hands—crafted a new table and a couple of benches for Dobah's imma. Miryam made herself useful as well, performing any task Imma asked of her, and Dobah's affection for her cousin's wife grew day by day.

Yeshua was adorable, as all babies were. He looked so much like Levi had only a year before, and Dobah loved to tend to Him, even though it made her wonder when or if she would have another child. Abba never spoke of arranging another marriage for her. She didn't know why. Perhaps he was waiting for her heart to heal. Or perhaps he liked having her and Levi in his home.

When the day of Miryam's purification and Yeshua's dedication arrived at last, the entire family set off together for Jerusalem, about an hour's walk from Bethlehem. Conversation and laughter filled the air around them, for this was a joyous occasion. Every firstborn in Israel, both human and animal, was dedicated to Adonai. The animals were sacrificed, but the humans were to serve God for the remainder of their lives.

Inside the city gates, the streets were crowded, and Dobah linked arms with Imma so they would not become separated. Leading the way, Abba carried Levi in his arms. At one point, the group stopped to purchase two turtledoves for Miryam's sacrifice then continued into the temple. Dobah's thoughts went back in time, to the day of her own purification after the birth of Levi. How was it possible that day passed so long ago and yet seemed like only yesterday?

A sound caught her attention, and she felt her eyes go wide at the sight of an unknown man taking Yeshua into his arms and holding him high. In a loud voice, he blessed God and said, "Sovereign Lord, as You have promised, You may now dismiss your servant in peace. For my eyes have seen Your salvation, which You have prepared in the sight of all nations: a light for revelation to the gentiles, and the glory of your people Israel."

Yosef and Miryam didn't move. Surprise—although not alarm—seemed to hold them in its grip.

The old man gave Yeshua back to His imma, saying to Miryam, "I am Simeon, and I ask the blessings of Adonai be upon you. This child is destined to cause the falling and rising of many in Israel, and to be a sign that will be spoken against, so that the thoughts of many hearts will be revealed. And a sword will pierce your own soul too."

Before any of them could absorb the words of Simeon, someone else approached. This time it was an elderly woman. Dobah recognized her as a prophetess called Anna, the daughter of Phanuel. It was known to those in Jerusalem and beyond that Anna served Adonai both night and day with fasting and prayers.

Placing a hand on the bundled infant, she began thanking God for Him and for the redemption He would bring to Israel.

What is happening? Dobah exchanged a look with her abba and saw her silent question mirrored in his eyes.

After a few more words of blessing, Anna turned and walked away, Simeon following behind her. Those who had stopped to watch shook their heads and moved on, the moment of interest already forgotten. But Dobah could not forget. It was all too strange.

"This child is destined to cause the falling and rising of many in Israel..."

The words resounded in Dobah's memory.

"...And a sword will pierce your own soul too."

Despite the warmth of the day, she shivered.

What does it mean? What does any of this mean?

Menes settled beneath the makeshift shade. It couldn't be called a tent. It wasn't as elaborate a shelter as the ones erected for the magi each day when they stopped to rest. But it was enough that he could sleep without broiling beneath the unrelenting sun.

During the more than six weeks of following the unusual light in the sky, he had learned the wise men knew more about their destination than they'd first revealed to him. Bethlehem in Judea, the Jewish Scriptures said, would be the birthplace of the new king. That was where they believed the star would lead them.

Menes was not an educated man, not in a formal way, but he had been taught to read and write, he was a good listener, and he absorbed the things he heard. He kept his mouth shut and his ears open. That habit had helped him become a sought-after khabir while he was yet a young man. And he had already learned a great deal as he listened to the magi talk. The men liked to debate fine points of the Jewish law, discussing whether or not certain words were prophetic. They talked about great civilizations, what had brought those civilizations to power and what had brought them down again. They spoke of the gods of Assyria and of Babylon and of Egypt and of Rome. Most of all, they spoke of the God of Israel.

So many gods. And of what use were they to anyone? A person prayed for rain and sacrificed to a god to make it rain, and if it didn't rain, if the prayer wasn't answered, a person simply repeated the sacrifices again and again, seeking to force the god's hand.

But as Menes listened to the magi, he began to learn that the God of Israel was purportedly different from other gods. That the God of Israel was a God who loved and cared for His people. A God who led them and guided them. A God who was their Good Shepherd.

Strange but intriguing claims.

CHAPTER THREE

In the cool of the morning, Dobah and Miryam walked together to the well. Several weeks had passed since the day of Yeshua's dedication and Miryam's purification, and little had been said about the extraordinary events of that day and all that had transpired at the temple. Perhaps no one knew what to say because they didn't understand what any of it meant. But there were times when Dobah looked at Miryam and believed her cousin's wife understood more than the rest of them combined.

As Dobah set her water jar on the stones next to the well, she said, "Abba is grateful for Yosef's help in the vineyards."

"My husband has been happy, lending a hand." Miryam smiled that shy smile of hers. "It is very different work from what he normally does, but he enjoys it."

Dobah laughed. "Imma will be sorry when you return to Galilee. The repairs Yosef has made around our house have needed doing for a long time."

Miryam filled her own water jar, and the two of them began the walk home.

"I suppose you must return to Nazareth soon," Dobah said.

"Yes. We have remained far longer than we anticipated when we came for the census. Yosef has arranged for us to travel with a family who has a donkey and cart. They are going north for a wedding in a couple of weeks."

"I wish you did not have to go."

Miryam stopped walking, forcing Dobah to do the same. "You have shown me great kindness, Dobah." She reached out and touched Dobah's arm with her fingertips. "You have been like a sister to me. I shall never forget it."

Dobah knew the whispers, of course. Even the distance between Nazareth and Bethlehem wasn't far enough to stop gossip from reaching them. But Dobah would never have believed what was said of her cousin, and now that she knew Miryam, she couldn't believe it of her either. Yosef and Miryam walked uprightly before Adonai. They kept the law of Moshe in their hearts and in their actions. It was a truth written on their faces and in their demeanors.

Dobah thought of the proclamation of Simeon in the temple, of the old man saying Yeshua was appointed for the fall and rise of many in Israel. What did those words mean? Were they a blessing or a warning? Could they possibly mean Simeon believed Yeshua was the Anointed One?

"Miryam, do you believe Yeshua will be…that He *is*…the Messiah?"

Something flickered in Miryam's eyes. Certainty. Confusion. Bravery. Fear. "He is and will be all Adonai appointed Him to be," she answered at last.

Which didn't really answer Dobah's question.

They resumed walking in silence, the two young women each lost in her own thoughts.

Star of Wonder: Dobah's Story

That night, after the entire household had retired, Dobah stood beneath the narrow window in her bedchamber, listening to the soft snores of her savta and the gentle tossing of Levi on his cot placed next to her own. There was a bright light in the sky that she had never noticed before. A strange light. What could it be?

"'When I consider Your heavens,'" she whispered, "'the work of Your fingers, the moon and the stars, which You have set in place, what is mankind that You are mindful of them, human beings that You care for them? You have made them a little lower than the angels and crowned them with glory and honor.'"

The words of her ancestor, King David, came easily to her tongue. All her life, her abba had repeated the songs to her, and she had memorized many of them, along with words from the Torah. She might not have been born a boy, but she loved Adonai and loved praising Him with Abba.

She focused on the heavens again. The bright light wasn't the moon. She knew that for certain. The moon had crossed the sky while it was still day. Was it a star? And if so, why was it so much brighter than all the other stars? Why had she never noticed it before?

The words of another song of praise came to her, and she spoke them aloud. "'He determines the number of the stars and calls them each by name.'" She rose on tiptoe, staring through the window. "Adonai, what is the name of that star? I would know it if I could."

"Dobah," her savta's sleepy voice came to her. "Go to bed. Your chatter is keeping me awake." Almost before the words faded, the old woman snored again.

Dobah looked once more at the light in the distance then went to her cot and lay down.

Adonai knew how many stars were in the sky, and He had named each one of them. The God of Israel was not distant as were the false gods. Adonai knew His chosen people, and like the stars, He called them by name. Abba said there were times when Adonai called a person's name twice, and always it was a show of intimacy, an example of how much He loved them.

Avraham! Avraham!
Ya'akov! Ya'akov!
Moshe! Moshe!
Sh'mu'el! Sh'mu'el!

Had Adonai spoken to her cousin in such a way? Had He called to Miryam? Surely He must have done so if they were the parents of the Messiah. Is that what made the couple seem different to her? Had they heard the voice of Adonai calling their names?

Living God of Israel, she mouthed silently, *would You call my name even once? I am listening. Let me hear You.*

The night remained silent around her, save for Savta's snores.

CHAPTER FOUR

The approach of the wealthy caravan to Jerusalem had, Menes was certain, been announced throughout the city for many days before their arrival. As had the wise men's question, "Where is the one who has been born king of the Jews? We saw his star when it rose and have come to worship him."

Emissaries of King Herod rode out to meet the caravan well before the camels stopped outside the gates of the ancient city. While the appearance of the king's guards made Menes anxious, the magi themselves seemed unperturbed. In fact, they seemed to have expected a welcoming committee.

As the magi were led away to dine as guests of the king, Menes cared for the camels and made certain the cargo went untouched by thieves. Every city had its share of robbers and pickpockets. Jerusalem was no different. But such men would not trouble *his* caravan. Menes was nobody's fool.

In truth, if not for the kindness of a neighbor, Menes might have become one of the thieves of a city back in Egypt. He'd been orphaned at a young age, before he'd begun to learn a trade. He could have been left to live by his wits. He might have starved to death before he'd reached the age of eight years. But Narmer, a man who lived next door to Menes's parents, had secured Menes a position on a caravan. Not as a slave but as an apprentice to the khabir. And so the gods had shown him favor. Or at least, that's what some had told him.

After many weeks of traveling through desolate country, the noise and bustle of Jerusalem made Menes wish he had time to explore. He didn't. There was no telling how long it would be before the magi returned. Perhaps a few hours. Perhaps a few days. He wondered if these wise men from the east knew the stories about King Herod and his murderous ways. Surely they must. The appointed king of Israel—a friend of Mark Antony—would not flinch from killing anyone he perceived as a threat. *Paranoid* was a word Menes had heard used to describe the ruler. But perhaps all kings were madmen. He did not know.

Menes sent a couple of men into the city to buy food in the markets. Not long after their return, he sat by himself in a place with a good view of his caravan and dined on fresh fruit and bread, flavorful cheese, and wine. He couldn't imagine that anything served in King Herod's court could taste any better than his own little banquet.

A glance at the sky told him there were still at least a few hours before the star would appear. He wondered what the people of Jerusalem had thought of it. When had it first been noticed by those in the city? Or was it not seen by everyone? Was that a possibility?

"Perhaps it is not a star," one of the magi had reflected recently. "Perhaps it is an angel of the Most High. What star or planet do you know that moves as this one does?"

His companions didn't have an answer to that question.

Menes leaned back on his forearms. An angel of the Most High. What did an angel look like? Just a bright light? Or like a beast of some sort? He hadn't a good enough imagination to conjure up anything in his mind.

He gave his head a shake. Better to think about the days ahead of him. If the magi's information was correct and the birthplace of this new king was less than a two-hour walk from where he sat, then this journey was nearly at an end for him. He would soon be paid most handsomely. He didn't doubt the magi wanted to hire him for the return trip to their homeland, but that had never been Menes's plan. He meant to find a replacement, another khabir who could take the magi back to their homeland. That shouldn't be difficult, given what they were willing to pay. And then Menes would be free to go to Egypt on his own. If that was still what he wanted to do. He wasn't sure. Perhaps now that he was in Israel, he should inquire of the God of the Jews what he should do. But Menes had never been a man of faith. He wasn't about to start pretending he believed now.

"What on earth is that noise?" Dobah asked as she placed hay in the mangers.

Although night had fallen, light spilled through the narrow windows of the house and over the gate of the stables.

"Camels," Abba said. "That is the sound of camels." He went to the door and opened it.

Dobah followed him there, and the sight that met her eyes made her gasp. Although camels were rarely seen in Bethlehem, it was not the beasts of burden causing her sound of surprise and amazement.

It was the men who rode upon them, and the bright light spilling over them from the heavens.

"Abba?" she said softly.

One of the extravagantly robed men approached. Her abba greeted him and the other men. Then, almost as if not of his own accord, he held the door open wide and stepped out of the way, allowing the strangers entrance. When the visitors saw Miryam with Yeshua in her arms, they dropped to their knees.

"Praise be to God Most High!" one of them declared, before lowering his forehead to touch the floor.

The others followed suit, including the men of humbler origins in their entourage.

"We have come to worship the King of the Jews."

Dobah felt her eyes widen even more. At the same time, she forced her mouth closed.

The first man who had entered the house straightened and looked over his shoulder then nodded at someone outside. Moments later, other men crowded into the room, their arms laden.

"Place them before the Child," their leader instructed.

They placed the gifts at the feet of Miryam and Yosef. Items of gold and bottles of precious oils. The house of Boaz ben David had never seen anything like these costly gifts. Gifts fit only for a king.

Dobah felt tears well in her eyes as she lifted Levi into her arms. "Remember this, my son," she whispered. "As young as you are, remember it all."

The richly attired men spoke words of thanksgiving and praise and bowed many more times. Throughout, Abba and Imma stood by, silent, watchful. Yosef's expression revealed some consternation.

And Miryam? There was the softest of smiles curving her lips, as if nothing could surprise her any longer.

Dobah didn't know how much time passed before the men rose to their feet, said words of farewell and additional blessings then backed out of the house. With their departure, the bright light vanished from the sky, as if God had blown out a candle in heaven. The camels outside grunted and hummed as the men remounted them, and soon the Bethlehem street beyond their front door had grown quiet again.

Abba stepped toward Yosef and Miryam. "Adonai must have a purpose, Yosef. I do not understand all that has happened, my nephew, but I know you and your wife have received a blessing from Yahweh."

CHAPTER FIVE

Dobah was awakened before dawn by troubled voices. She slipped from beneath the light blanket on her cot and went to the door of the bedchamber. Several oil lamps illuminated the living area of the home, the light revealing Imma, Abba, and Yosef putting Yosef and Miryam's belongings, along with food and the gifts they'd received, into cloth sacks. Two donkeys stood in the stable, packsaddles awaiting the supplies they would carry. Babe in arms, Miryam stood against the wall where she'd sat only hours before when the men from the east came to worship her infant son.

"Abba?"

He looked at her. "Come and bid your cousin goodbye, Dobah."

She moved into the center of the room, her gaze traveling between Yosef and Miryam. "You are leaving? Now? Before daylight?"

Yosef came to her and took hold of both her hands. His dark eyes looked deep into hers. "Believe me, Dobah, when I tell you. An angel of Adonai came to me in a dream. He told me to get up and to take the Child and His imma and flee to Egypt because King Herod is going to seek to destroy Him."

"Why would a king want to kill a baby? Why would he harm Yeshua?" She looked from Yosef to her abba and back again. "And why would the angel send you to Egypt? Why not go home to Nazareth?"

"I do not know the answers to your questions," her cousin said. "I only know we cannot tarry. We must be away as quickly as possible, and we must go where He sends us." He hesitated a moment before adding, "Perhaps you and Levi should come with us."

"Why should we leave our home?"

He shook his head. "I cannot explain. It is a feeling I have. You should not be here. There is danger. You and Levi are not safe."

Abba's arm came around Dobah's shoulder. "She will stay with us. We will protect her."

Yosef didn't argue. He squeezed Dobah's hands before releasing them and hurrying to finish the packing.

"Abba, where did you get the other donkey?"

"It belongs to Barak. We will buy him another."

"We will need to buy two if we are to replace our own."

"We will use the gold your cousin is leaving for us."

She looked toward the stable. Of course. She'd forgotten the wealth that had been spread before Yosef and Miryam last night. Wealth that they would now need in their hasty flight to Egypt.

You and Levi are not safe." She shivered as Yosef's words whispered in her memory.

Abba took hold of Dobah's elbow and steered her toward the steps leading down to the stable. A short while later, she stood between her parents at the stable gate, watching as her cousin and his family were swallowed up by the night.

"How would Herod even know about Yeshua?" she asked softly.

"The magi found him here. The king will know of it soon enough."

She looked at her abba. "Are we in danger, as Yosef said?"

"No." He made a scoffing sound.

But was it meant to reassure Dobah or himself?

Late in the afternoon, with his payment from the magi carefully hidden upon his person and his remaining camels stabled with a man he'd known for many years, Menes made his way to Bethlehem, drawn there by a need he could not define. Perhaps he needed to remind himself of what he had witnessed the previous night. Perhaps he needed to understand why his knees had seemed to buckle before an infant, why words of praise could not be contained in his throat.

There was no star to guide him today, but he didn't need one. The streets he and the magi had passed through seemed burned into Menes's memory, and he found the modest home on the western side of Bethlehem without much effort. His knock on the door was soon answered by a woman in her forties, a woman who had been present when the magi arrived. He'd noticed her briefly, but then he'd seen nothing but the young couple and baby. He'd heard nothing but the words of the magi.

"I am Menes," he told the woman then gave a respectful nod. "I am the khabir who brought the magi to your door."

She looked beyond his shoulder. "Have they returned?" There was a note of hope in her question but perhaps some fear as well.

"No. They...they chose not to return to Jerusalem." Should he tell her of the dream one of the magi had had? The dream the wise man swore God had used to warn them to return to their homeland by another way.

A sound from the street drew Menes around, and he saw a tall, broad-shouldered man open the gate to enter the small courtyard. It was clear by his demeanor that this was his home. Menes gave a slight bow and repeated the words he had told the woman moments before.

"I am Boaz ben David, and this is my wife, Machla. You are welcome to our home, Menes."

"I am grateful for your hospitality."

Inside, he discovered a young woman of perhaps nineteen or twenty years, an elderly woman with a face as wrinkled as a prune, and a toddler of about a year old or so who walked, mostly on tiptoe, about the living area of the house. But the couple and baby he had seen the previous night were not there. When he asked about them, he was met with silence and worried glances.

He lowered his voice. "Has something happened?"

Boaz seemed to measure Menes with his gaze, and Menes hoped he wouldn't be found wanting in the older man's estimation. Why it mattered, he couldn't say. But then, much of what had happened of late was beyond his ability to explain.

Boaz lowered his voice to match Menes's. "They left Bethlehem. They were warned that King Herod meant the Child harm."

"Warned in a dream?" Menes asked.

Boaz's expression darkened with suspicion.

"Because that was how the magi were warned. In a dream, they were told not to return to Herod. They were sent back to their own country by another way."

"And you did not go with them?"

"No."

"Why?"

"From the outset of the journey to Bethlehem, as we followed the star, I had planned to leave the magi once they found their king and go to Egypt, the land of my birth."

"Egypt," Boaz repeated softly.

"But first," Menes continued, "after I saw the caravan on its way with a new khabir, I felt... I felt compelled to return to your home. I thought it was to see the infant king a second time, but perhaps I was mistaken."

"You are welcome to stay with us, Menes. The guest room is empty now."

The Jews were a hospitable people. Menes had learned this through the years. Their God called upon them to be kind to strangers in their midst. Even so, Boaz's invitation caused Menes to look at the man in surprise.

"I cannot explain it," Boaz said, "but I believe it is Adonai's will."

Menes gave his head a slight shake, not knowing what to say.

Boaz placed his hand on Menes's shoulder. "The purposes will be made clear to us. I have seen too much in recent weeks not to believe it."

CHAPTER SIX

Dobah wasn't certain what to think of Menes, the Egyptian camel driver. More than a camel driver, according to her abba. A khabir. An expert at leading caravans across vast stretches of land. A man who knew where to find water when the lack of such knowledge would mean certain death. She had seen him with the magi the previous night. She had watched him bow down alongside the wise men from the east and express devotion to the infant in Miryam's arms.

But why had Abba invited this stranger to stay in their home? It wasn't as if Menes couldn't find lodging elsewhere. He must have the resources to stay anywhere he chose. Why here?

As they ate their simple supper that evening, Dobah watched Menes and listened as he answered Abba's and Imma's questions. There was no denying he was handsome. He was tall, like her abba, with a lean, muscular build and wavy black hair. He had strong, well-defined features—a sharp jawline and a straight, prominent nose. Although no more than five years her senior, something in his large brown eyes told of the rugged life he had lived, and made him seem older.

But it was his infrequent and fleeting smile that Dobah noticed most. When he smiled, it was as if something melted inside of her.

As the meal drew to a close, Levi left her side to toddle over to Menes. There, he studied Menes as openly as Dobah had studied him covertly. After what seemed a long time, Menes responded with laughter. Even as the sound faded, his smile lingered on his mouth and a sparkle shone in his dark eyes. The feeling that flooded through Dobah made her face grow warm. She quickly lowered her gaze to the floor lest someone notice her reaction.

What was wrong with her? This feeling couldn't be attraction. It *mustn't* be attraction. Menes was a foreigner. He wasn't a Jew, and even more, he wasn't a believer in Adonai. But then she recalled him, kneeling with the magi, his forehead pressed against the floor. Menes had bowed low before Yeshua whom the visitors from the East had declared a king. Dobah had not bowed. More than once, she had stood back and questioned all she had seen and heard over these past weeks, from the day of Yeshua's dedication in the temple to last night, when that bright star in the heavens had shone down upon this ordinary house in Bethlehem.

Who is the unbeliever here? Menes or me? The questions that whispered in her heart unsettled her and made her want to go somewhere and hide.

Levi returned to her, and she drew her son onto her lap and pressed her cheek against the dark hair on his head. He squirmed, forcing her to draw back. With his small hand, he patted her cheek. "Imma," he said.

Love welled and tears stung her eyes. Jewish girls knew their calling was to marry and have children. But nothing had prepared Dobah for the way she would feel about her son. From the first moment she'd held him, she'd known this love was something special, almost indescribable. Were her emotions for Levi heightened because of Dover's death? Or would she have felt the same way even with her husband at her side?

Imma began to clean away the remains of the evening meal. Dobah helped her, but as soon as all was finished for the night, she slipped outside, Levi riding on her hip. The evening air was cool, and Bethlehem had fallen into silence. Stars sprinkled the black sky overhead, but that unusual star, the one that had led the magi to this village, was gone. Dobah wished she could see it one last time.

From inside the house, she heard Abba invite Menes to join him at the vineyard in the morning, and Menes agreed. Again, Dobah wondered why he was here, why her abba treated him in much the same way as he'd treated Yosef. Menes wasn't family. Menes wasn't even a friend. He was a stranger. What made Abba do what he was doing?

Eyes on the heavens again, she whispered, "Nothing makes sense anymore."

Dobah ran, clutching Levi to her chest. Steep cliffs rose on both sides of the valley, looming over her in the darkness. A hand pressed against the small of her back. A strong hand. A man's hand. She wanted to turn to see who was running beside her but was kept from it by an unseen force.

Fear tightened her chest, making it hard to breathe. Somewhere behind her, evil was in pursuit. She tasted blood on her tongue and heard cries of terror in the dark. Her feet felt heavy, as if she were dragging weights. But panic kept her moving forward, running toward safety.

A full moon suddenly appeared in the night sky, larger than any moon she'd ever seen. Even so, she stumbled over a large stone and pitched forward. The man at her side caught her and kept her upright.

But the evil had come closer. She felt it nipping at her heels, like a hound at the hunt.

"Adonai, help us!" she cried.

With a gasp, she sat upright in her bed, breathing hard, the terror remaining even as the nightmare faded away. Heart in her throat, she reached out in the darkness to touch her son on his small cot next to her own. He was sprawled sideways on his bed. Needing reassurance, she placed her hand on his chest and felt the steady beat of his heart. It soothed her a little...but not enough.

She rose and went to the window. It wasn't all that long ago that she'd seen the bright star in the night when looking out this same window. Now the sky was dark. The night she'd first seen that unusual star, she'd prayed for Adonai to speak to her, to call her by name. Was this dream His answer? Was it a warning like the one given to her cousin?

Yosef's words echoed in her memory. *"Perhaps you and Levi should come with us."*

Was it only the bad dream that made her wish she'd accepted her cousin's invitation?

"An angel of Adonai came to me in a dream."

There'd been no angel in her dream. Hers was no more than her imagination. Perhaps caused by something she'd eaten.

A shudder ran through her, and she returned to her bed, dread following her there.

CHAPTER SEVEN

Even two days later, Dobah's nightmare clung to her, never giving her rest. She didn't speak of it to anyone. What could she say? It was only a bad dream. Everyone had them at one time or another. And yet...

Dusk was falling over Bethlehem as the family prepared to eat their evening meal. But before Imma and Dobah could carry food to the table, a cry drew their attention toward the street.

"Boaz!"

Abba rose from the bench and hurried to the door.

"Boaz!"

Abba disappeared through the doorway. A moment later, Menes followed him. Dobah exchanged a look with Imma.

"Boaz!" The man's voice was closer now. "Herod's soldiers. They are here!"

Heart racing, Dobah went to the door and looked outside. The man in the street was a good friend of Abba's. He leaned his hand on the stone fence, terror written on his face.

"Herod's soldiers. They are looking for baby boys. They are slaying the sons of Bethlehem. They are coming this way."

Dobah heard the words, and the fears that had lingered from the nightmare crashed down upon her, like a great weight from the sky. *"Why would a king want to kill a baby?"* Her own words, spoken to Yosef days before, taunted her.

"Protect them if you can," Abba's friend said. Then he ran down the street toward his own home.

Her abba, usually a man who liked to ponder and consider and weigh every option, sprang into action. "Machla, get food for them. Dobah, grab clothes and blankets for you and Levi. Menes—"

"I will take them," Menes said. "We will find her cousin and family."

"But—"

"We will find them, Boaz. I know the way to Egypt."

Dobah expected her imma to protest. This man was a foreigner, almost a complete stranger. That he would take responsibility for the daughter and grandson of Boaz and Machla made no sense. That they would race off together in the night seemed an impossibility.

A scream rent the night air, and it sent an icy chill through Dobah's veins.

This was not just any night, and their flight was not for an ordinary reason. Saving Levi was first on Imma's mind, just as it was Abba's and Dobah's.

They heard more screams as Dobah hugged her parents goodbye. Imma kissed Levi's head. Abba did the same before passing his grandson to Menes to carry.

"We must go," Menes said. "Now." He left the small yard.

Dobah and her abba followed. Ahead of them, Menes ran with her son, Levi, cradled in his arms. Evening was quickly turning into a moonless night. And darkness was what they wanted. The darkness provided their best hope of escape from the terror sent by

King Herod. Panic kept Dobah's feet moving, even as her lungs cried for relief.

"Menes," Abba called softly after they left the village behind them.

The young man slowed, looked back, and then stopped.

"Take them to safety." Abba held out a bundle to Menes. Inside was food and perhaps some funds for the journey. Only what a few moments had allowed Imma to throw together. "Do all you can to protect them."

"I will."

The two men clasped wrists, their gazes locked in the moonlight.

"They are precious to us," Abba added.

"I know, Boaz. I will protect them with my own life."

"It is a great deal for me to ask of you."

"I believe this is why I am here. Your God brought me to Bethlehem for this moment."

Abba released Menes's wrist and pulled Dobah into his arms. He kissed the top of her head. Then he gently pushed her away. "Go. And may Adonai go with you. Do not forget to follow His ways."

Tears caused his image to wave before her.

"Dobah," Menes said, "we must leave now."

Would she ever see Abba and Imma again? Would she ever again sit beside the cook fire in the home where her abba had been born and where she had been born and where Levi had been born?

"Dobah!" The urgency in Menes's voice spurred her into action. Clutching her small bundle against her chest, she followed the former khabir away from the road and into the rugged hill country that surrounded the only place she'd ever called home.

Menes held Dobah's arm as they scrambled down another hillside in the dark. They were far enough away from Bethlehem now that they no longer heard the cries of despair rising in the night. But it wasn't far enough for Menes to believe they were out of danger. He didn't know if Herod's soldiers were searching the countryside for more children to slaughter. Had they been told where the baby named Yeshua had been born? Did they care how many innocents would perish this night when that Child was long since on His way south?

Reaching the bottom of another steep hillside, Menes said softly, "We will rest for a while."

Menes was used to traveling at night, and his vision had adjusted to the darkness. He saw Dobah hold out her arms. Without hesitation, he passed Levi to her.

Dobah lowered herself to the ground. "You have been so good, my son," she whispered.

"He has been good." Menes leaned against the rock wall at his back. "Not a sound, all this time. Not even while a stranger carried him." Although he didn't know a lot about babies or small children, Menes guessed Levi's silence throughout their flight from Bethlehem had been nothing short of a miracle.

"You are not a stranger any longer. Levi knows you. Remember how he looked at you as we ate two nights ago? He knows you better than I do."

Menes slid to the ground. "You may ask me anything you wish."

His words were met with silence. No doubt, she thought it improper to be the one to ask questions of a man. Especially one who wasn't a relative. Menes may have spent the majority of his life traveling with men and working with camels, but he wasn't completely ignorant of proper behavior around women.

"Perhaps you would tell me about your husband."

More silence followed. But Menes was a patient man, and he waited.

At long last, speaking softly, she said, "His name was Dover ben Natan. His father also owned a small vineyard. We knew each other almost our entire lives." She paused then added, "He was a good man."

"I have only known your father a few days, but I know he would not have allowed you to marry a man who was not good." Was it possible to hear a smile? It seemed to Menes that he could hear hers, and he was encouraged. "Boaz is a good man too. I learned much from him in the days we worked together."

"Abba loves meeting new people. He would have asked you many questions even as he taught you how to tend the vineyard."

"Yes, he asked many questions. Perhaps that is why he entrusted you and Levi to my care." Menes nodded into the darkness, as if confirming the words to himself. "The magi spoke often of the Living God of the Jews. Two of them had studied the Torah and other writings of your people, and what I heard them say during our journey and what I saw that night in Bethlehem is what brought me back to your door."

"Abba called it Adonai's will."

"Do you believe that as well, Dobah?"

"I do not know what to believe anymore."

He heard the troubled tone of her voice and decided it was better to be silent. At least for now. "We will rest a short while longer. Then we should try to put more distance between us and Bethlehem."

"Dobah."

The hand on her shoulder shook her gently.

"Wake up."

Her eyes flew open. The sky overhead remained dark, but there was a thin strip of light on the horizon. Morning was not far off.

"You let me sleep." Her tone was almost accusing. She drew a breath and added, "Thank you."

"We need to go as soon as you and Levi are ready."

Only then did she realize Levi was no longer in her arms. When had he escaped her embrace? How long had he been exploring in the night? She couldn't believe it hadn't brought her instantly to her senses. He might have been snatched away by a wild animal or fallen into a hole.

Adonai, preserve us.

She leaped to her feet. In the dim premorning light, she searched for the toddler. He wasn't far off as she'd feared. He stood behind Menes, trapped between the man's legs and a large boulder. A sigh of relief escaped her lips.

After finding a place of privacy to relieve herself, she washed Levi in a nearby stream—little more than a trickle of water—and dressed him. They had limited clothes with them, and she wondered how she would keep the little boy clean during the journey ahead. She'd traveled to Bethsaida years ago, but having been a child herself, she hadn't thought about how to stay clean.

After breaking their fast with bread and cheese, they set off. Dobah carried Levi against her chest in a sling, and he seemed content, his eyes exploring the passing countryside, occasionally jabbering but mostly silent. Menes set a brisk pace, his eyes constantly searching the land. By midmorning, with Bethlehem far enough behind them, they walked on the road, blending in with other travelers headed south.

Around noon, they rested and ate more of the bread and cheese Imma had sent with them. But when they were finished and returned to the road, Menes started back in the direction they'd come from.

"Where are we going?" Dobah asked in a low voice.

"To a place outside of Jerusalem."

Her pulse quickened. He wanted to go close to the city where King Herod lived? She thought they were running away from him and his murderous soldiers. "Why would we go there?"

"For my camels. I left them with someone I trust."

"But—"

"Camels are valuable, Dobah. I must sell them and buy us some donkeys and a cart. It is a long way to Egypt."

Buy us... The words felt strangely intimate.

"Menes, why are you doing this? For me and Levi. For my family. Why are you putting yourself at risk?"

He met her gaze, his expression solemn. "I cannot explain it. I only know it is something I must do. I must take you to your cousin in Egypt. If the Living God sent Yosef and Miryam there to keep

Yeshua safe, then you and Levi will be safe there as well. Your son will not be safe in Bethlehem. Perhaps not anywhere in Israel. Not as long as Herod lives."

Her throat tightened and her eyes misted. All she could do in reply was nod.

CHAPTER EIGHT

The right wheel of the cart dropped into a rut, jarring Dobah's teeth. The pain in her head and sheer weariness made her want to weep, and this was only two days after they'd left Jerusalem with two donkeys—one to pull the small cart and one as a spare—and enough supplies to hopefully see them through the journey. Or maybe it was knowing it would take nearly a month to reach Alexandria that brought on her sorrow.

"About twenty-five days," Menes had told her, "including rests for Shabbat."

She hadn't told him she couldn't travel on Shabbat, but he had known and intended to honor the religious observance, despite the danger that was part of each day. Bandits were Menes's main concern. Being alone on the road put them at greater risk. On the other hand, she was a woman traveling with a man who was not her husband. There was risk to her reputation in that. Should someone ask, they had decided to say Menes was a friend of her abba's, escorting her to family in Egypt. They need not say the friendship had been formed mere days before nor that the family she was to join wouldn't have reached Egypt yet themselves.

Her gaze went to the donkey pulling the cart and to the man who walked beside the animal, lead rope in hand.

Menes never seemed to rest. He remained alert as he walked and when they stopped to rest and eat. Even when he slept, he seemed ready to leap to his feet at the slightest sound. He carried two knives. She had seen the weapons, and she had no doubt he knew how to use them.

"There will be water ahead," Menes said, turning his head to look back at her. "We will rest the animals there and eat something. How is Levi?"

"He is asleep."

"After we rest and eat, he can ride on the donkey if he wants."

"He will want. He loves it." She thought she would also prefer riding on the donkey to riding in the cart, although she hadn't ridden one since she was a young girl. Her imma had forbidden it once she'd come of age.

She turned her face upward, taking in the blue sky dotted with puffy clouds. There was no rain in them, which was good. Of course, if it rained, they could take cover beneath the cart. But it was a small cart, and the three of them would be in tight quarters if they had to shelter there. The thought of lying that close to Menes, even with Levi between them, made her stomach tumble.

Dobah remembered the nightmare from five nights ago. There'd been a man beside her in the dream, guiding her along the treacherous trail. Had the man in the dream been Menes? Had Adonai sent her the dream to prepare her for this very journey?

She shivered. It was difficult enough to believe the Living God would speak to Miryam and Yosef through the visitation of an angel, something they had both claimed. And they were the parents of the Messiah—or so it seemed. But it was impossible to believe

Adonai would speak to her in the same way. To Dobah, the daughter of Boaz ben David. She was no one. A Jewish widow from Bethlehem. Her husband had not been a man of wealth or influence or power. When Dover died, Dobah had been left dependent upon her abba. She always did her best to be a good Jew, to honor Shabbat and observe the festivals and say her prayers. But still, she was a woman. A woman of no importance.

But was Miryam that much different from Dobah or Dobah from Miryam? Was Yosef so different from Dover or her own abba? Miryam and Yosef were poor people from a small village. Yosef was a craftsman as his father had been before him. He built things with his hands. Still, until the visitation from the magi, her cousin had been able to afford nothing more than a pair of turtledoves for the sacrifice at the temple. For Dobah's purification the previous year, Abba had purchased a sheep.

And yet Miryam had been chosen to be the imma of the Messiah.

Could that possibly be true? Were the magi right? Were Miryam and Yosef right? Or was this all a strange madness?

That night, they camped once again without the company of other travelers nearby. Menes found a site off the main road, hidden from view by the terrain. Their dinner was dried fish and fruit. Menes felt secure enough to build a fire to ward off the chill of the night air. Dobah was grateful for that, although the shadows that seemed to move about in the darkness continued to make her nervous.

I wish I were home in my own bed.

"You are sad," Menes said in a low voice.

She looked at him, seated on the opposite side of the fire. "I miss my abba and imma. I even miss Savta's snoring."

He chuckled.

"Well, maybe I do not miss that."

After a lengthy silence, Menes said, "I remember the first time I journeyed from home. I was only a young boy, and I did not leave a warm and loving family behind me. Still, I longed for the familiar. It will get better with time."

"How often do you return to your home?"

"I have no home to return to. I was a small boy when I was orphaned. After my parents died, all that they had was taken away. I had an uncle in Alexandria, but I do not know if he is there still."

"I am sorry, Menes. That you were orphaned as a boy. That must have been hard for you." Tears welled in her eyes, her thoughts once again returning to the parents and grandmother she'd left behind. "Do you suppose they are all right? Abba and Imma. Did the soldiers leave them alone?"

"Herod's men would have had no reason to bother them once you and Levi were gone."

"What if the soldiers were told there was a young boy in their house? Our neighbors knew about Levi. They knew about Yeshua too."

Menes shook his head. "I do not know everything about your people, but I know they do not hold King Herod in high regard. I do not imagine your neighbors would tell his soldiers anything, as long as they could keep from doing so."

As if from a great distance, she recalled the cries she had heard that night. "Why did he do it? Why did he kill them?"

"I heard rumors in the city when I sold my camels. They say the king went into a rage when the magi did not report back to him. I was told he sent his men to kill all the boys in Bethlehem, two and under, because any of those boys might have been the new King of the Jews the magi went looking for." He lowered his voice to just above a whisper. "They say the king fears everyone and is willing to kill anyone he thinks might try to take his place."

Dobah lifted Levi into her lap, disturbing the toddler's quiet play. He objected by wriggling in her arms and releasing a cry that split the night air. She released him to return to the toy on the ground.

Menes rose and stepped away from the fire. Did he watch for enemies who might have heard Levi?

As she waited, holding her breath, she heard Abba's voice whispering in her memory. *"'Why, my soul, are you downcast? Why so disturbed within me? Put your hope in God, for I will remember you from the land of Jordan, the heights of Hermon—from Mount Mizar. Deep calls to deep in the roar of your waterfalls; all Your waves and breakers have swept over me. By the day the Lord directs His love, at night His song is with me—a prayer to the God of my life.'"*

"Hope in God," she said softly. Her gaze fell to Levi, playing quietly once more. "We must always hope in Adonai and keep His song with us like a prayer." How she wanted to feel the confidence those words were meant to inspire within.

She wondered what her life would be like, far from Abba and Imma, far from Bethlehem. She would not be near the temple and would be unable to make sacrifices or attend the festivals. Would they be able to find Yosef and Miryam, or would she never see family again? Would there be a synagogue where they were going? Would she know others who worshiped the Living God?

Questions tumbled in her mind, and she longed to lift her son into her arms and draw comfort from him. But he was barely a year old. He had no idea what his imma wanted and couldn't give it anyway.

Hope in God, her heart answered again.

"Dobah," Menes said from out of the darkness. "You should try to get some sleep."

She wondered if he would do the same.

CHAPTER NINE

Menes had learned early in his apprenticeship with his first khabir that it was the sameness of the days—one after another after another after another—that made a journey hard. It wasn't the threat of bandits or the danger of venomous creatures or the occasional attack by a wild animal that made the trip difficult. It was one day being so much like the last and one meal being so much like the one before it.

Eight days after he'd led Dobah away from Bethlehem, the one thing Menes could say that made this journey better than any other was the sun. He liked traveling in the daytime instead of at night. Add to that a slower pace, meant to ease things for the mother and child, and he decided the next couple of weeks would be more bearable than most. He was also thankful for the times when they had been able to travel with a few others. But those companions had been temporary, none of them going as far as him and Dobah.

It was late in the afternoon, and Levi was seated on the donkey that was pulling the cart, his mother walking with a hand on the little boy's back to keep him steady. Once again, it was just their own small party on this stretch of road. That's when two men appeared around a bend. They looked to be in their thirties or forties with long beards and traditional attire. Nothing about them looked like men who lived in the wilderness, supporting themselves by stealing from travelers. Nonetheless, Menes stopped the donkey.

"Dobah, take Levi and stand behind me." He spoke in an even tone, not wanting to alarm her or the boy.

She didn't question the command but obeyed quickly.

He wished now they had waited and not pushed on until they'd found another group headed south. Perhaps one bound for Egypt. His hand went to the dagger beneath his cloak.

One of the men looked up and noticed them. He raised an arm and called, "Greetings."

The back of Menes's neck tingled. Something didn't feel right, but he couldn't say what.

Perhaps he would have found out, but from behind him came the sound of cantering hooves. The men in front of Menes exchanged a look and then darted back the way they had come. Menes turned to watch the approach of a Roman patrol. Not a surprise. Few but Romans had horses. There were ten riders. The one in front raised a hand, and the men behind him slowed their horses to a walk then halted when the *decurion* came up beside the cart.

From the corner of Menes's eye, he saw Dobah had pulled her headscarf forward, concealing most of her face. Even so, her head was ducked down, and she held Levi close against her chest, making them both appear as small as possible. Good. She was right to be cautious.

Menes gave a respectful bow and waited in silence.

"Where are you headed?" the Roman asked.

"South, my lord. To Egypt. My home."

The decurion's gaze flicked to Dobah then to the rear of the cart, and finally to Menes again. "There have been reports of bandits along this stretch of road. Have you seen any signs of them?"

"We have had no trouble, my lord, and we have seen few other travelers today." He thought of the two men who had hurried out of sight at the approach of the patrol. Part of him wanted to tell the decurion what he had seen. Another part—the prudent part—thought it better to remain silent. In his experience, Roman soldiers were often no more to be trusted than thieves and robbers.

"It would be best if you and your family traveled with others."

Regarding traveling with others, Menes was in complete agreement. "Yes, my lord." He dipped his head again.

The decurion glanced back at his men and motioned with a hand as he barked an order. In unison, the riders spurred their horses into action. Dust rose in a cloud behind the patrol, and Menes turned his back to the road, waiting for it to settle.

After a lengthy silence, Dobah said, "I was afraid they were looking for us."

"I do not believe anyone is looking for the daughter and grandson of Boaz ben David. We are too far from Bethlehem. And that man"—he looked toward the bend in the road—"thought you were the wife of an Egyptian. Others will think the same." When he turned toward Dobah again, he found her blushing, her eyes averted.

She was innocent to the world beyond Israel, and he was charged with keeping her safe. No matter what, he must keep his promise to Boaz. His job was to take her to Yosef and Miryam. He would do whatever was needed to accomplish that goal.

"The decurion was right," he said. "The dangers will increase. There is desolate land ahead of us. We must find others with the same destination and join them."

"How do we do that?"

"This road meets another that has more traffic. We will reach it tomorrow, and we will find company. I am sure of it."

He was sure of no such thing. But he hoped his words would prove true.

Dobah had known, of course, that the people they'd met over the past week assumed she was the wife of Menes. They'd assumed Levi was his son. It wasn't an unreasonable assumption, and the belief provided a level of protection. It shouldn't make her feel this uncomfortable, hearing Menes say the same, but it did.

With each passing day, with the ever-increasing distance between them and Bethlehem, the fear that King Herod and his assassins remained a threat lessened. But the dangers to travelers on the roads remained as real as ever. She and Levi were still in need of safeguarding. She'd seen those two men on the road ahead before the soldiers arrived. She'd sensed Menes's wariness, had seen his hand touch the dagger at his waist, had wondered if more men lay in wait beyond the bend.

Perhaps Adonai had sent the Roman patrol to protect them. It would not be unlike the Living God to use those who did not know Him for His own purposes. But would He do so for her? She was no one of importance. But once that thought entered her head, she could not shake it. Didn't want to shake it. The idea that the Living God of Israel might care enough for her and Levi to send a Roman *decurion* to save her from a band of robbers. It defied belief. And yet...

"Up ahead," Menes said, breaking into her thoughts. "That is where we will stay for the night."

She blinked, surprised it was time to make camp already. Then she realized how much lower the sun was in the sky than it had been when they encountered the Romans. How long had they walked while she was lost in thought?

The smell of the sea wafted to them on a breeze. They were close to it, but the terrain hid it from view. Close to the Mediterranean Sea but far from Bethlehem and Jerusalem. Perhaps not even in Judea any longer.

Homesickness hit her like a blow to the abdomen, and she sucked in a breath as her vision blurred.

"Are you all right, Dobah?"

She turned toward the man who had so willingly taken on the role of her protector. A man who had treated her with respect and great care. Who showed kindness to her son, even when Levi got tired and cranky. He was not an Israelite. He was not a Judean. But was he a believer in the Most High? Her abba must have believed Menes a proselyte of Adonai or he never would have entrusted his daughter and grandson to him.

"I am all right," she answered at last. "Only tired and hungry."

Again the breeze brought a whiff of the sea, and she found herself wishing for some fresh fish to cook over the fire. Perhaps in the next few days that was something Menes could make come true.

CHAPTER TEN

It was midmorning the following day when Dobah felt hope wash over her as travelers on an adjoining road came into view. There appeared to be several families in the group, which comforted Dobah even more.

Please, Adonai, let them be going to Egypt.

Menes hailed them while still a short distance away. He stopped the donkey and handed the lead rope to Dobah then walked toward the other men.

Please be going to Alexandria. She glanced down at Levi, sleeping now in the sling. *Menes says Alexandria is where we will search for Yosef and Miryam first. Let these people be going there too.*

After a short conversation, Menes looked over his shoulder toward Dobah and gave the smallest of nods. She couldn't help smiling as she led the donkey forward.

"We have been invited to join them, Dobah," Menes said. "Our destinations are the same."

There appeared to be three families. The three men were young, and they were similar enough in appearance for her to believe they were brothers or cousins. She spied *tzitzits* hanging from their garments and knew the men must be observant of the law. Behind them stood an elderly woman, her hair gray and her face lined, reminding

Dobah of her savta back in Bethlehem. The other women, three of them, looked to be in their twenties, not much older than Dobah herself. Several children scampered around a cart pulled by a donkey, and several more rode in the back of the cart. Two of the women had infants in slings.

If they were to travel with these people the rest of the way to Alexandria, she would surely have to explain she was not Menes's wife. It was one thing to let a Roman cavalryman think they were married. It was something else to try to fool several Jewish families for better than two weeks. That would be lying to them even as they got to know one another. No, that would not do at all.

As the travelers joined the main road, Menes and Dobah fell in behind the others. Walking on the opposite side of the donkey from Menes, Dobah said softly, "We will have to tell them."

He looked over the back of the jenny. "Tell them?"

"That we are not man and wife."

"Ah. Yes. We will need to tell them that. I am a friend of your father, doing him a favor by escorting you to your family in Alexandria."

Was that also a lie? It didn't seem so. In only a couple of days, Menes and Abba had grown close. And when Herod's soldiers came to Bethlehem, Abba had not hesitated to entrust his daughter and grandson to Menes. As for her family being in Alexandria, that was not so much a lie as hope.

Yosef hadn't said where they planned to go when he told Dobah of the angel's command. He was to take the child and His mother to Egypt. But Egypt was, Menes had told her, a large country. There were many places Yosef and Miryam might go within those borders. But what Menes did know for certain was that there was a large

Jewish community in Alexandria. It made sense to assume that Yosef would go there first, even if they didn't remain long.

Dobah saw one of the younger women—the one not carrying an infant—look back at them, and then she slowed her pace and moved to the edge of the road, obviously waiting for Dobah and Menes to catch up with her.

She offered a shy smile as she fell in beside Dobah. "I am Noa, wife of Shimon."

"I am Dobah. And this is Levi."

"What takes you to Egypt?"

"We go to find my cousin and his family. I...my abba thought it would be best for us." She glanced toward Menes, knowing she must speak the truth now. "My abba asked Menes to escort me and my son."

Curiosity filled Noa's eyes, but not censure. "He is not your husband?"

"No. Levi's abba is dead. He died before seeing the birth of his son."

"How very sorry I am for you."

Dobah lowered her eyes. "Thank you."

Softly, Noa began to recite, "'The Lord is my shepherd, I lack nothing. He makes me lie down in green pastures, He leads me beside quiet waters, He restores my soul. He guides me along the right paths for His name's sake.'"

Dobah joined her voice to Noa's. "'Even though I walk through the darkest valley, I will fear no evil, for You are with me; your rod and Your staff, they comfort me. You anoint my head with oil; my cup overflows.'"

They paused in unison, their gazes meeting. Then they continued, "'Surely Your goodness and love will follow me all the days of my life, and I will dwell in the house of the Lord forever.'"

The donkey huffed, and the cart wheels creaked. Otherwise, the world seemed to have gone silent.

"Amen," Dobah added.

The smell of the sea was even stronger that night.

"Will we see it soon?" Dobah asked Menes as he unhitched the donkey from the cart.

"The sea? Yes. Tomorrow the road will follow in sight of the shore. It will be so for a few days only. Then the road will take us farther south."

She could almost smell fish cooking. Wait. She *could* smell fish cooking. She turned in a circle, looking for another campsite, for a fire and fish.

Menes laughed. "I would like the same."

He'd read her mind. It seemed he often did so.

"I will see if I can find the source." He tethered both donkeys where they could forage for food, and then he moved toward Shimon and the other men. Soon the four of them set off down the road, leaving the women and children to prepare for the night to come.

It seemed a long time passed without their return. So long that Dobah became anxious. Had they run into trouble out of view of their camp? How many other people were around the next rise or the next bend in the road? Were they good people or bad people? Were they Romans or bandits or fellow travelers?

Even though I walk through the darkest valley, I fear no evil, for You are with me.

Throughout her childhood, Abba and Imma had taught Dobah many of the songs written by the great king of Israel. She would do well to remember more of those songs when her heart was troubled. And since she was running away from Israel, going to a foreign land to live among people who worshiped foreign gods, a troubled heart might be more common than not.

Dobah scooped up her son as he walked too close to the campfire Noa had made then carried him to where the donkeys grazed. Once there, she closed her eyes and recalled the final words of another song she had learned from her abba.

But I trust in Your unfailing love; my heart rejoices in Your salvation. I will sing the Lord's praise, for He has been good to me.

A sense of peace warmed her chest. For she knew without a doubt Adonai had dealt bountifully with her too. If Yosef hadn't received a dream in the night, if Menes hadn't come to Bethlehem, if Abba hadn't understood the dangers at the first news of the soldiers, then Levi might not be alive in her arms tonight. She and her son had experienced the salvation of El Shaddai, and she would sing to Him. She would remember Him in the night whenever she was afraid.

"Ho! Dobah!"

She opened her eyes and turned toward the sound of Menes's voice. He had one arm raised, and in his hand he held a large fish. A large *fresh* fish. Her mouth watered at the sight. A blessing from Adonai, to be sure.

CHAPTER ELEVEN

Levi's soft voice, chattering to himself, awakened Dobah from a pleasant dream. She opened her eyes to find a blue sky beyond the entrance of her tent, the dark of night having been driven away by the rising sun. For a moment, she feared she had overslept. Then she remembered it was Shabbat. They would not travel today. She relaxed against the blankets on the ground.

Menes had told her they were in Egypt now, having left the land of the Nabateans behind them. In another week, they would arrive in Alexandria. And then what? Would they find Yosef and Miryam and their baby there or would they have to search elsewhere?

She shivered. Yesterday, she'd heard one of their fellow travelers, Hoshea, say Alexandria held the largest population in the world, as much as five times that of Jerusalem during one of its festivals. Perhaps even larger. Her mind couldn't take in how many people that must be. The city of Jerusalem overwhelmed her, even at nonfestival times. Even if Yosef and Miryam were there, how would they find them?

"I will trust in the name of the Lord our God," she whispered.

"Mens!" Levi squealed, bouncing with excitement.

Dobah rolled her head to the side and looked through the opening again. Menes was up and adding fuel to the fire, a chore prohibited to Jewish men on Shabbat. He moved with ease, showing no signs of weariness after nearly three weeks of travel. In truth, he looked handsome and—

"Mens!" her son called again.

This time, Menes looked toward her tent. She doubted he could see her or Levi since they were in shadow, but he smiled anyway. Then he held out his arms in invitation. A strange warmth coiled in Dobah's stomach, and she wished she could run to him the way her son did now, bursting out of the tent and making his way to Menes as fast as his chubby little legs could go. Her face warmed as she sat up, pushing loose hair off her forehead.

It wasn't possible. These feelings welling inside of her couldn't be what they seemed. It truly wasn't possible she should feel anything more for Menes than gratitude. He was a kind, good, and brave man who had helped her escape with her son because he'd been present at the right moment. That was all.

Abba's parting words played in her memory. *"May Adonai go with you. Do not forget to follow His ways."*

Dobah closed her eyes and whispered her morning prayers, promising in her heart she would never forget Adonai's ways, no matter how far she traveled from Bethlehem and Jerusalem, no matter how far away she was from Abba and Imma and Savta. And no matter how strong her attraction to an Egyptian khabir might grow.

Help me, Adonai.

Menes sat near the campfire, adding fuel when required. The others, being Jews, weren't allowed to light a fire on Shabbat or to cook any food. It was possible that even keeping the flame going wasn't allowed by Jewish law, although no one said anything to Menes. Perhaps because he was Egyptian and not bound by their law.

After breaking their fast with foods prepared before sundown yesterday, the group sat in a circle, talking and sharing stories, sometimes repeating words from the Torah they had put to memory. As he had done with the magi, Menes listened to what they had to say, taking it all in and hoping to learn from it.

For nine days he and Dobah had traveled with these three families, and Menes had come to respect each one of them. Both the men and the women were kind and hospitable. The men treated their wives with tenderness and weren't afraid to show love to their children, although they could be stern as well. That they loved and sought to obey their God was obvious, much as it had been with Boaz. It had surprised Menes to discover how much he wanted to be like Boaz.

His gaze traveled across the campfire to where Dobah sat with the other women and the children. Levi played with one of the other boys, a lad around his age. The boys squealed their laughter as they patted their hands on their thighs. Menes wasn't sure who the other toddler belonged to. Hoshea and Penina? Shimon and Noa? Amos and Yiska? Menes couldn't keep any of the children straight, except for Levi.

He smiled to himself. Levi had become a part of his own heart over the last three weeks. Something Menes had never expected. His profession had scarcely put him in the company of children. He'd determined to return to Egypt, to find a wife and start a family. He hadn't pictured himself with those future children. He hadn't imagined holding one of them on his knee or laughing as he watched them play. Being with Levi had changed that.

His gaze went to Dobah again, and he realized his recent thoughts of marriage and family had a great deal to do with her as well as Levi.

God of Israel, would Dobah have me for a husband? Would her family allow it? I am a foreigner among Your people? I have seen Your Messiah with my own eyes, but I am ignorant of Your ways. Teach me Your ways.

The prayer was strange to him. Throughout his life and travels, he had never put faith in any of the gods he had heard about. Not in the gods of Egypt. Not in the gods of Syria or Arabia or Mesopotamia. But he knew now that the God of Israel was the one true God. Adonai lived, and He had sent the Messiah, a Savior for His people. A Savior for all peoples. If he knew nothing else, he knew that much, and he would cling to the belief even as he sought to learn more.

"Ah, and Boaz married Ruth. What of that?"

Hearing the name of Dobah's father pulled Menes from his thoughts.

"Ruth was not merely a gentile, Hoshea. She was a Moabite. The Moabites do abominable things in the eyes of the Living God. And yet Adonai made her the great-grandmother of King David. He changes the faithless into the faithful."

So Shimon was not speaking of Dobah's father. It was someone else.

"May I ask," he said into a temporary silence, "who is this Boaz and Ruth?"

The eyes of the others around the fire turned upon him.

Star of Wonder: Dobah's Story

Shimon smiled. "It is good for you to ask, Menes, for it is a story I love to tell. It begins with a famine in the days when the judges governed Israel. A man named Elimelech from Dobah's own city of Bethlehem left Israel with his wife and two sons and went to dwell in Moab, on the east side of the Jordan."

"A poor decision," Amos said.

Shimon ignored the interruption. "Then Elimelech died, leaving his wife, Naomi, a widow with two sons. And the sons took for themselves Moabite wives. Their names were Orpah and Ruth. They lived in Moab for ten years, and then both of Naomi's sons died, like their father before them."

Shimon was an excellent teller of stories. His voice could soothe or excite, and did both during his recitation. As Menes listened, he felt a kinship with Ruth the Moabite woman, a gentile who found faith in the Living God, a foreigner who became a part of the history of Israel. Perhaps, if such a thing could happen to her, then it wasn't beyond the realm of possibility Menes might be able to do the same. Perhaps it might also mean he could win the affection of Dobah.

CHAPTER TWELVE

Eight days later, on the outskirts of the sprawling city of Alexandria, Dobah and Menes bid farewell to their traveling companions. Tears welled in Dobah's eyes as the women exchanged hugs. These people had made her feel safe, and now she didn't know if she would see them again after today. Not in a city of this size.

As if reading Dobah's mind, Noa said, "Perhaps we will attend the same synagogue. There are several of them in the Jewish quarter, I am told, but maybe we will share the same one once we are settled."

Settled? How could she be settled without her parents, without her sisters and their families? How could she be settled away from Bethlehem?

Soon the three other families moved through the gates of the city and were swallowed up in the throngs of people.

"How do we find Yosef?" she whispered.

Menes answered, "He has the gifts given to them by the magi. They will not be homeless. And Yosef is a *naggara*. Every city looks for artisans. We will find them. Even among a Jewish community as large as this one, someone will know where they are."

"They did not say Alexandria was where they would go."

"I know. You told me. But it is logical they would do so. Your father thought so. We spoke of it when I worked with him in the vineyard."

Nerves swirled in her stomach. She wanted to tell Menes her abba had never traveled farther than the Sea of Galilee, so how could he know what was logical in Egypt? But to do so would sound critical of her abba, and she didn't want to do that. Especially now, when she might never see him again.

The tears returned, and this time they flowed freely.

Menes's hand alighted on her shoulder. "It will be all right, Dobah. Your God has preserved us this far."

She nodded, her throat too thick to voice a reply.

"Then let's go." Menes led the donkey toward the gate, and they joined the flow of people going into the city.

It was the sounds Dobah noticed first. Voices speaking languages she didn't understand. Many voices, varied languages. A loud cacophony. Next came the scents of spices and foods offered for sale by street vendors, along with odors not as pleasant from the droppings of animals. As they moved deeper into the city, she began to marvel at the architecture and the huge buildings.

Seeing a tall structure in the distance, she asked, "What is that?"

Menes followed the direction of her eyes with his own. "The Lighthouse of Alexandria. It serves as a beacon for ships navigating the harbor." He stopped and looked about then said, "Wait here."

A twinge of alarm shot through her, but she relaxed when she saw him take no more than a half dozen steps away from her. He spoke to two men on the side of the street, and she could see they understood one another.

"Thank You, Adonai."

From the sling, Levi tipped his head back to look at her. With a laugh, he reached up to touch her lips, as if he understood her words of thanksgiving. She laughed with him.

Menes returned. "I have directions to the Jewish quarter." He pointed. "We have to make our way there. Should we get something to eat?"

"Oh, please. I am hungry, and I imagine Levi will get fussy if he does not eat soon."

Menes grinned. "We will move in the direction of the Jewish quarter and get something along the way. I am sure we'll have many opportunities. If I remember right, we will go through the *agora*. There will be plenty for us to buy there."

Plenty for them to buy. The words caused a stab of guilt. Yes, Abba and Imma had sent her away with what little funds they could spare, but in truth, this journey had been taken at Menes's expense. He'd sold his camels. He'd bought the two donkeys and the cart. He'd paid for the supplies that had kept them warm at night and fed in the day.

"Menes." She touched his wrist then withdrew her hand quickly, embarrassed by how intimate the gesture felt. "You have done so much for us. You have spent so much of your own money to get us here. How shall I ever repay you? I am not—"

"Dobah, I do not expect to be repaid."

"But—"

"I believe I was in Bethlehem for this very purpose. I cannot explain it and yet I believe it." He took a half step closer to her, his head leaning forward, his gaze holding hers. "I have never been a man of faith. I had no use for any god. But I followed that star. It was no ordinary light in the sky. I know the stars. I have traveled by them all my life. That was not just any star. Stars do not travel. And I was there when the magi knelt low and worshiped the infant in Miryam's arms. I heard their praise. Those were learned men who came to see a King." His voice deepened. "And I knew then that Adonai *is* God, and He brought me to your family for a purpose. This is my purpose."

She had followed the ways of Adonai all her life. She had been raised to keep the law and to worship El Shaddai. And yet in this moment, she saw that Menes's faith was greater than hers.

He took a step back, another smile playing at the corners of his mouth. "Come. We will eat and then we will find Yosef and Miryam. Adonai has kept us safe and brought us this far. He will see us through to the end."

Dobah continued to be overwhelmed by the opulence and decadence of the city they moved through. They found food in the public market, just as Menes had said they would. But the meal did not sit well in her stomach as they passed in the shadows of the temples dedicated to Serapis and other false deities, and when she saw the theaters and gymnasiums and public baths. She had heard of similar cities, of course. They could be found throughout the Roman Empire, including in the Decapolis on the eastern side of the Sea of Galilee. But she had never thought she would walk through the streets of one and see such things for herself.

It was a seeming change in atmosphere that told her they had arrived in the Jewish quarter. There was less noise here. While the streets were busy, the area seemed less boisterous, more industrious. But it was the sight of *mezuzahs* on doorframes that confirmed her feelings were correct.

The homes were densely packed. In addition to single-family dwellings, there were multistoried buildings that she assumed held several apartments. Some buildings were simple, made of mud bricks. Others were homes for the wealthy.

Menes didn't stop to speak to anyone as they passed through a residential district. He seemed intent on going deeper into the quarter before he began to inquire about a young family, newly arrived from Bethlehem.

Dobah didn't object. She felt intimidated by the street they followed, a street that never seemed to end. Jerusalem had nothing to compare to this. Not in size. But Jerusalem had the temple, and that made it a city beyond compare.

Oh, but she longed to look upon the temple again.

In that moment, her gaze alighted on a large building a short distance down the street. Made of stone, it had columns and ornate friezes, making it similar to other buildings she had passed on the way to the Jewish quarter. But this building had a menorah carved into the wooden door at the entrance. There was no mistaking that this was a synagogue.

Her pulse quickened. "Praise be to Adonai."

Menes glanced over at her.

"The synagogue," she said, louder this time. And in her heart she added, *We can be at home here.*

CHAPTER THIRTEEN

Dobah awakened the following morning in a small room at an inn. She felt a little lost at first. It was odd not to be inside her tent or lying beneath the cart. Beside her, Levi still slept. Apparently he too liked the feel of the bed beneath them instead of hard and lumpy ground. She rolled onto her side and snuggled close to her son's small body. Love welled inside her. In her memory, she heard again the distant cries of women whose sons had been taken from them by Herod's soldiers, and tears came to her eyes and dripped onto the bed.

Adonai, thank You for sparing him. Comfort those who have lost much.

Even as she prayed, she wondered why she had received Adonai's mercy. Why her and not another? Then she thought of Miryam and wondered the same. Why her and not another?

As if in answer to her silent question, she remembered the rabbi reading from the scroll of Isaiah. *"For My thoughts are not your thoughts, neither are your ways My ways,"* declares the Lord. *"As the heavens are higher than the earth, so are My ways higher than your ways and My thoughts than your thoughts."*

"I never once asked any questions," she whispered, wondering why she hadn't been more curious.

She hadn't asked Miryam how or when she knew the child she carried would be the Messiah. She hadn't asked about His conception or the night of His birth. She hadn't asked about Miryam's feelings after the encounter with Simeon and Anna at the temple. She hadn't asked anything, really. Why not?

Perhaps because she still couldn't believe it was true. Yosef was her favorite cousin, but he was an ordinary man. He was poor—or had been until the magi came with their gifts. He had begun working with his abba at a young age. Although a craftsman, his life had been a simple one without any promise of great change. How could Yosef raise the Messiah? What made him worthy of such a thing? And Miryam. She was a simple girl from a poor family in Nazareth. Why would she be chosen to be the imma of the long awaited Messiah?

Levi stirred and, moments later, opened his eyes. When he saw her watching him, he grinned.

"We must wash and change you," she said to him. "The day is waiting."

A short while later, the morning ablutions completed for both herself and her son, Dobah was moving toward the door to the room when a knock sounded, followed by Menes's voice. "Dobah, are you awake?"

"We are." She opened the door. "I did not know we had slept so late."

"That does not matter. I have news. I may have found Yosef and Miryam."

She felt her eyes go wide.

He nodded. "It is true. This morning, as soon as the sun was up and people were about their business, I went out into the street and talked to people there. And one man told me he knew someone who had hired a recent arrival from Israel to make repairs to his home. He could not be certain, but he thought the naggara's name was Yosef."

Could it be as easy as that? In a quarter that held, she'd been told, close to a hundred thousand Jews? Could they really find Yosef and Miryam in only a day?

"My ways higher than your ways and My thoughts than your thoughts."

A shiver passed through her.

"As soon as you and Levi have something to eat," Menes said, "we will see if this naggara is truly the one we seek."

"I think it will be him," she said softly. "I think it must be them."

Dobah and Menes left the inn, Levi in Menes's arms. The sun shone down upon the busy thoroughfare, painting the buildings in golden rays. Women stood before shops and stalls. Men conducted business outside doors and at the corners of buildings. Children played on rooftops overlooking the street. A dog dug in the dirt near the corner of a house.

It wasn't long before Dobah spied another synagogue, this one as large as the one she'd seen yesterday. The Jews of Alexandria must be faithful to Adonai, even surrounded by the temples and practices of idols. That comforted her. At least a little.

Eventually, Menes stopped to speak to a merchant selling cloth. The other man listened then pointed. Menes thanked him.

"This way," he said to Dobah, and they set off again, turning right at the next corner.

This street was narrower than the last. Fewer people traversed its length. Bathed in shadows, it reminded her of a street in Jerusalem. Soon, homes gave way to a small commercial district. Shops lined the street, and Menes slowed his pace, his eyes looking through open doorways. And then he stopped.

"There. Look." He pointed.

Just outside the doorway of a shop, she saw two grinding stones.

"I think that is the place."

Dobah gave Menes a questioning glance before following him through the open doorway. She looked around the dim interior. This shop had obviously been in business for a long while. Tables and shelves held more grinding stones, several mortars and pestles, and many other household tools and utensils. Had Yosef found employment with the owner?

"Hello?" Menes called.

From an adjoining room, came the reply. "I am coming."

Her heart fluttered. It couldn't be. She had wanted to believe. She had believed. And yet...

Yosef appeared in the opening to the other room, wiping his hands on a towel. Surprise widened his eyes. "Dobah?"

"Yes." She smiled weakly. "It is me."

"But when? Why?" Yosef's gaze went to Menes, obviously wondering who he was.

And why would he know him? Menes had been an observer behind the magi on that momentous night. Which seemed strange to Dobah now, after so much time in his company. In many ways, it seemed she had always known him.

"There is much to tell you, Yosef," she said.

"Boaz? Machla? They are well?"

"They were when I left them."

"How did you find us?"

It was Menes who answered. "Adonai provided." He bowed his head briefly then introduced himself.

Yosef's eyes flashed in recognition. "You were with the magi."

"I was."

"How is it you are with Dobah now?"

Dobah stepped forward and placed her hand on her cousin's forearm. "The story is long. But Levi and I"—she glanced over her shoulder at her son, still safely held in Menes's arms—"are well because of Menes. And if you will have us, we have come to make our abode with you and Miryam."

"Of course we will have you." Yosef drew her into a warm embrace. "It is our deepest wish. Come. I will take you to Miryam."

"She is nearby?"

"She is upstairs in our new home above my workroom."

Dobah drew back. "Your home? Yosef, you arrived not many days before us. Do you tell me you already have a home and business in Alexandria?"

Her cousin smiled. "I do. As Menes said, Adonai provided. There was a widow who wanted to sell immediately, and I wanted to buy and had the means to do so because of the gifts of the magi."

Dobah's thoughts whirled, leaving her dizzy.

"Where are you staying now?" Yosef asked.

She told him of the inn where they had spent the night.

"We will go for your belongings after you have seen where you shall be staying. And Miryam and I must hear what brought you to us."

With an arm still around her shoulders, Yosef guided her through the doorway to the opposite side of a work area. Stairs led to an upper room. He allowed her to precede him while Menes and Levi followed behind.

"Miryam," Yosef called a moment before Dobah's head rose above the floor of the second story, "look who is here."

Dobah saw Miryam turn and watched surprise and joy blossom on the young woman's face.

"Dobah? Is it really you?" Miryam met Dobah at the top of the stairs and hugged her tightly.

"It is me," she answered, just as she had answered Yosef a short while before.

"Come. Do you need something to eat or to drink?"

"No. Thank you. We ate not long before coming to look for you."

The apartment above the shop and workroom was well furnished, giving it a long-lived-in appearance. The widow must have left everything behind in the sale of her late husband's business and their home.

Menes was introduced to Miryam, and Levi was turned loose to run about and burn off some pent-up energy. Dobah had a few moments to admire Yeshua, who slept peacefully in a basket in a corner of the room.

"Oh, how He has grown," she said.

"Yes. He did not seem to mind the weeks of travel. He is a good baby." Miryam motioned for Dobah to sit. "Please. Tell us what brought you to us."

Dobah drew a breath. "When Yosef said there was danger in Bethlehem, he was right. It arrived only a few days after you left us."

And then she and Menes told them what she knew of the evening Herod's soldiers had come to the sleepy village.

CHAPTER FOURTEEN

Menes was reunited with his grandfather's elderly cousin, Seti, the next afternoon. The old man lived on the side of Alexandria opposite the Jewish quarter, miles away from Dobah and Levi. There was no great warmth shared between Menes and his cousin. They had met infrequently over the past two decades whenever Menes's caravans brought him to this city built on the shores of the Mediterranean Sea. It didn't help that Seti—Menes's only living relative, as far as he knew—could have taken the young orphaned boy into his home but had chosen not to.

But Menes had not returned to Egypt to reunite with an elderly cousin. He had returned with the intention of finding a wife. And whenever he thought of that, Dobah's image came into his mind. No matter what he did, his thoughts strayed to her and Levi again and again. He wasn't concerned about their welfare, of course. They were safely at home with Yosef and Miryam. They no longer needed his protection. It was he who was in need.

And so, three days later, he set out across the city to see how they were. As on the day of their arrival, the streets of the Jewish quarter teemed with life. The same as the rest of the city he'd walked through. The same and yet different.

Because of the God they worship.

The thought had no sooner entered his mind than he saw the synagogue. Almost of their own volition, his steps carried him toward the entrance to the large building. Passing through its doors, he was conscious of the eyes watching him. He stepped off to one side, certain someone would come to speak to him before long. And he was right.

"What is it you want?" a stern-faced man in dark robes demanded.

"I wish to speak to a rabbi."

The other man raised bushy brows.

"Please."

"Wait here."

Menes was glad to stay where he was. In fact, it gave him time to leave, if he wanted. Perhaps he didn't belong. And yet he remained.

Soon another man in dark robes approached. This one had a friendlier appearance behind the long gray beard. "I am Chizkiyahu. How may I help you?"

Menes bowed his head respectfully. "My name is Menes." He took a slow breath and released it. "I have come to believe Adonai is the only true God. I wish to receive instruction in the Torah so that I might follow His path."

Chizkiyahu smiled, a look that reached his eyes. "You are welcome, Menes. Come. We will sit and talk a while."

Dobah sat on the rooftop, enjoying the cooling breeze from the sea. It reminded her, as so many things did, of Menes. She remembered him, holding up a big fish when they were near enough to the sea that he could buy the fresh fish for their evening meal. That memory triggered others, moments of kindness, moments of bravery, moments of wisdom, moments of faith.

A lump formed in her throat. She tried to tell herself it was caused by homesickness. And that much was true, as far as it went. She missed her abba and imma. She missed the quiet streets of Bethlehem. She missed seeing all the familiar faces at the synagogue on Shabbat. But it was Menes she missed the most. Would she see him again? Was he still in Alexandria or had he left the city? Her heart twinged at the last thought. Surely he wouldn't go without telling her farewell.

Levi toddled over to her and patted her knees with the palms of both hands. "Mens! Mens!"

Tears stung her eyes. Even her son was thinking of Menes, missing Menes.

A sound from the steps leading to the roof caused Dobah to quickly wipe the tears from her eyes. Then she leaned over the hand mill and continued to grind the wheat.

"Dobah," Miryam said as she approached the bench, "you have not stopped working since you rose this morning."

"I rest whenever I watch Levi at play."

Miryam sat beside her on the bench.

"Yeshua is sleeping?" Dobah asked.

"He is."

"And Yosef?"

"He has been hired to work on a large home outside the Jewish quarter. Already his skills have been recognized and are in demand."

"Yosef was always talented with his hands. Even as a boy, working with his abba."

Miryam laughed softly. "It does not hurt that we came to the city and immediately bought a business and home. Others think it is because Yosef was so successful in Israel. No one knows it is because of Yeshua and the magi who came to worship before Him."

Dobah stopped grinding the grain between the two stones and straightened. Her gaze went to Miryam. "When did you know?"

"Know what?"

"When did you know Yeshua was the promised Messiah?"

"I was told by an angel that I would bear Him."

"An angel?"

"Gabriel, a messenger from Adonai." Miryam closed her eyes, the smile lingering on her lips. "'Do not be afraid,'" he told me. "'You have found favor with God.'"

A shiver passed through Dobah, for it seemed she heard the words in a voice that was somehow more than Miryam's own voice.

"I was perplexed," Miryam continued. "What sort of greeting was that which had been spoken? And then the angel told me I would become pregnant and that I would name my son Yeshua." She opened her eyes and looked directly at Dobah. "And he told me that Yeshua will be great and will be called Son of Ha'Elyon. He will be given the throne of His forefather, David, and there will be no end to His kingdom."

"How can this be?" Dobah whispered.

"That was my question too, since I was a virgin. And he told me the *Ruach HaKodesh* would come over me, and the Holy Child born to me will be called the Son of God."

"Miryam, I do not understand what that means."

"Neither did I. But I answered Gabriel, 'I am the Lord's servant. May your word to me be fulfilled.' And he left me." Miryam paused then added, "It all came to pass, just as he told me it would."

"And Yosef?"

Miryam gave her head a little shake. "Yosef might have ended our betrothal when he learned I was with child, but he too received a visitation. The angel told him not to be afraid to take me as his wife, for what was conceived in me was from the Ruach HaKodesh. He told Yosef that Yeshua would save His people from their sins."

"It is all so hard to believe."

Miryam laughed again. "Even for me. Even now. I walk around in a state of amazement. I do not know why I was so favored by Adonai. I do not know what it means that Yeshua will one day save His people from their sins. He is a baby, in the way of all babies. He is hungry and He eats. He is tired so He sleeps. He cries and He needs changed. And yet…"

"And yet wise men came to worship Him."

"Yes. And shepherds too."

"Shepherds?" Dobah shook her head. "What shepherds?"

"On the night Yeshua was born, shepherds came. They appeared at the stable entrance in the deep of the night. I heard one of them say, 'The Child is here.' I was alarmed, but Yosef went to ask what they wanted. I will never forget the reply." Miryam closed her eyes. "'We are shepherds,'" the man said, "'who keep watch over the flocks. Tonight was a night like every other until suddenly an angel appeared to us. The glory of Adonai shone all around him, around all of us. The messenger told us not to be afraid and declared that in

Bethlehem this night we would find a Child wrapped in cloths and lying in a manger. He said it would be a sign for us that a Savior has been born, a Savior who is the Messiah, the Lord.'"

Dobah whispered, "Even poor shepherds knew."

"Even the shepherds."

"And then Herod wanted to kill Him."

"Yes."

Dobah reached out and touched Levi's cheek. He giggled then toddled toward the toy he had dropped earlier, a small block of wood with markings carved into its sides. Yosef had given it to Levi the previous night.

Miryam reached over and took hold of Dobah's hand. "Adonai alone knows what tomorrow may bring. But He will keep us."

"On our way to Egypt, we traveled with a small group of other Jews bound for Alexandria. One of the women reminded me of the songs of King David that I learned from Abba and Imma as a girl. I want to remember more of them. Perhaps you and I could practice them together?"

"I would like that, Dobah. I would like that very much."

CHAPTER FIFTEEN

Days passed without any sign of Menes. Too many days.
Yosef worked every day except on Shabbat. When he wasn't called to work in another part of the city, he labored in his own workroom below the living quarters, fashioning items to be sold to customers. Miryam and Dobah attended to their sons, cleaned the house, washed the clothes, cooked the meals. Dobah was always made to feel welcome. She never felt like a burden or a guest. She had been taken under her cousin's wing. She lived under Yosef's protection and was a member of his family. That was all good.

But there were moments when she felt utterly and completely alone. She was a foreigner in a foreign land, no matter that she lived in the Jewish quarter. She longed for Israel. She longed for home, for the place she truly belonged. But most of all, she missed Menes.

How ungrateful she must be. Adonai had protected Yosef and Miryam and Yeshua. He had provided for them abundantly. And because He had protected and provided for them, in His mercy He had done the same for Dobah and Levi.

One morning, as Dobah returned from the well with a full jar riding on her shoulder, she looked up in time to see Menes enter the doorway to Yosef's shop. Her heartbeat quickened first, and then so did her steps. It was a wonder she didn't drop the water jar in her excitement. Menes had come. He hadn't abandoned her.

She knew then what she felt for him. She had learned to love this man during the journey from Bethlehem to Alexandria.

Her footsteps slowed.

Her abba had trusted Menes to take her to safety. But would he approve of his daughter's feelings? No. She thought not. Menes was not of her people. She had known her husband for much of her life, long before she had known she would become his bride. She had known Dover's parents and his grandparents. Dover had learned the Torah at his abba's knee, the same way Dobah had. He had worshiped at the synagogue with Dobah and her family.

She stopped in the doorway to the shop. Menes stood in the shadows of one corner, talking to Yosef. She must have made a sound, for both men looked in her direction at the same time.

Menes smiled that warm smile of his. "Good morning, Dobah."

"Menes." She nodded before moving into the shop.

"You look well."

"I am well. Thank you."

He took a step toward her. "I was hoping we could speak together."

Yosef said, "Dobah, take the water up to Miryam, please. Menes and I will follow soon."

Dobah's pulse pounded in her ears for a different reason now. She felt afraid. Afraid of what it meant, that Yosef was sending her away when the person she'd longed for finally stood before her.

"Dobah," Yosef added, his voice soft but firm, "we will not be long."

She felt the heat rise in her cheeks as she hurried through the doorway to the workroom and then up the stairs.

Miryam looked up as she laid Yeshua in His basket. Her eyes widened. "Is something wrong?" She straightened.

"No." Dobah hurried to the table and set down the water jar. "Dobah?"

She shook her head. "Menes is here. He and Yosef are talking."

"Oh."

Miryam's single word seemed to speak volumes. Had the young mother guessed Dobah's feelings for Menes even before Dobah had known them herself? "Where is Levi?" she asked, suddenly needing to look at her son.

"He fell asleep while you were gone." Miryam pointed toward the sleeping chamber Dobah shared with Levi.

Dobah walked to the doorway and looked into the room at her son. He lay on the cot on his side, sucking his thumb, a habit he had formed in recent weeks. Perhaps it was the stress of their flight from Israel, although he hadn't shown it. He had been such a good boy during the journey, rarely complaining in even the slightest manner. Nonetheless, he was too young to understand everything that had happened, and his ability to communicate with Dobah was limited.

"Do you wish you could go home?" Miryam had come closer, and she asked the question in a low voice.

"How will we know when it is safe to do so?"

"Adonai awakened Yosef in the night to tell him we had to leave Israel. He will tell us when it is time to go home."

A lump formed in Dobah's throat. "What if He never tells Yosef it is time to go?"

"Adonai promised He would, and He is a promise keeper."

Oh, for the faith to believe that.

"Yosef tells me there is a line in the scroll of the Prophet Hosea that says, 'Out of Egypt I called my son.'" Miryam glanced over her shoulder toward the basket on the floor where Yeshua slept peacefully. "In time, He will call us out of Egypt, for His Son is here now, and His work is in Israel among His people."

"You are so sure."

"There are many things I am unsure of, Dobah, but I am sure of that."

Footsteps on the stairs caused both women to turn around. Yosef appeared above the stairway, but Menes didn't follow.

"But I—" Dobah started to say. The she pressed her lips together.

Yosef met her gaze with a tender one of his own. "Menes has gone for now, but he will return. I believe you can be sure of that."

"But he said he wished to speak with me."

"He did. He still does. But the time is not right, Dobah. Not yet."

"I do not understand."

His expression grew stern. "In the absence of your abba, I must see to your interests."

Her cousin's words didn't surprise her. And in most regards, she would have welcomed them. She had been under the protection of her abba, then her husband, then her abba again. And now she was under Yosef's protection. He was her nearest living male relative in Egypt. It was as it should be.

Except…she'd wanted to talk to Menes, and that choice had been taken from her.

Menes left the Jewish quarter, his spirits downcast. He'd wanted to talk to Dobah, to tell her of his meetings with the rabbi and the instruction he was receiving. He wanted her to know his faith in Adonai was not temporary but lasting. And he wanted her to know of his hopes for the future, a future where the three of them—him, Dobah, and Levi—were together.

But Yosef had understood Menes's intentions without explanation, and he'd sent him away. "For now," Yosef had said. "It is too soon and much is uncertain."

Perhaps circumstances were uncertain, but Menes himself was not. He knew what he wanted, and he would not be turned away for long.

On the same day Menes had gone to the synagogue for the first time and spoken with Rabbi Chizkiyahu, he had left Seti's home and taken an upper room in a house just outside the Jewish quarter. In the ten days since then, he had not only begun his studies in the Torah, he had considered what he would do to make a living. He'd known nothing but life as a camel driver and khabir. He'd been successful leading caravans across many nations. Financially, he was neither poor nor rich. Nor was he used to being idle. He must work at something, and if he wanted a wife and family—and he did—he would prefer not to be away from his home for the better part of every year as his lifelong profession required. Was it possible for a man of his age to become an apprentice in an entirely different trade? And if so, what would that be?

He thought of Yosef, who worked with stone and wood. His own son, Yeshua, would one day join him in the workroom, no doubt, but that was years away. He might be glad for a man to work with him. Could that man be Menes, despite how little he knew?

Reaching his destination, Menes climbed the stairs on the outside of the house to his small upper room. Once inside, he sat on a stool near the lone window and looked outside. All he could see was the wall of the house next door, but still he stared through the opening. Silence surrounded him, the sounds from the street fading into nothing. Then into the silence came words he had memorized in the past two days. Words not from the Torah but the songs of a king.

"'Blessed is the one who does not walk in step with the wicked or stand in the way that sinners take or sit in the company of mockers, but whose delight is in the law of the Lord, and who meditates on His law day and night. That person is like a tree planted by streams of water, which yields its fruit in season and whose leaf does not wither—whatever they do prospers.'" Calm seemed to flow over him as he recited the words aloud. "I will delight in You," he added, "and on Your law I will meditate. Plant me by Your stream, where I may prosper for You."

CHAPTER SIXTEEN

"Dobah!" Miryam's excited voice rose from the workroom.

Fear jumped into Dobah's throat as she hurried to the top of the stairs. "What is it?"

"You have a message from your abba."

"Abba." The name came out on a breath. Nearly two months had passed since she'd last seen her parents. She hadn't known if she would hear from them ever again.

"Come down, and Yosef will share it with you. I will keep an eye on the children."

"They are both still sleeping." Dobah hurried down the steps and through the workroom, barely giving Miryam a glance as she passed her.

Yosef stood in the center of the shop, listening intently to the older man who was with him. Yosef's grave expression caused Dobah to stop in the doorway between the two rooms on the ground floor. As eager as she was to receive her abba's message, she sensed all was not right.

The older man nodded, bid Yosef *shalom*, and left the shop. Yosef stood looking after him for what seemed an eternity. But at last he turned. When his gaze met with Dobah's, the look on his face caused her heart to squeeze.

"Abba? Imma?" she whispered.

"I am told they are well."

She leaned against the wall as she released a breath.

"Come. Sit." He looked down at the parchment in his hand. "We will read the message together."

Dobah had always struggled with reading. No doubt her cousin remembered that about her. They each sat on a stool, and Yosef unrolled the parchment. The message was short and to the point. Abba and Imma missed her and Levi. They were well. They prayed for her and their grandson every day and hoped Adonai would bring them both back to Israel soon. They were entrusting the message to a wine merchant known to her abba who was traveling to Alexandria, and they prayed it would reach her and find her well. They hoped she would be able to send them news, if someone could be found to carry the message.

Dobah wiped away tears. "That is all it says?"

Yosef let the parchment roll close again. "That is all."

"Then why do you look so grim?"

He closed his eyes for a moment. "Because of the news that came with the message."

She waited, her hands clenched in her lap.

"Of all the sons of Bethlehem under the age of two who were in the village on that day…only Levi survived Herod's soldiers."

Images flashed in Dobah's mind. Friends from synagogue. Young wives and their baby boys and young toddlers. Pudgy legs and curly dark hair and giggles. Dobah raised her hands and pressed them against her chest, as if to keep her heart from breaking.

"Levi could have been murdered too," she said softly.

Yosef raised his eyes, as if to heaven. "It was Adonai's will that your son would be saved."

"Yes. And Adonai sent Menes with the magi so he might lead us out of Bethlehem and bring us to you."

Her cousin nodded. "Adonai is merciful."

Her thoughts momentarily turned from her abba's letter and the news from Bethlehem, Dobah asked, "Why has Menes not returned to this house? Did you tell him he would not be welcome?"

"He is not one of our people, Dobah."

"He believes in Adonai. He came to believe on the night the magi visited you and Miryam and left gifts for Yeshua."

Her cousin nodded again. "So he said to me."

She wanted to tell Yosef she loved Menes, but of course, she couldn't. It wouldn't be proper. And besides, she didn't know if Menes wanted to marry her. He had taken care of her and Levi, bringing them safely to Alexandria, but he'd made no promises beyond that. But still her heart hoped.

Dobah had been in Alexandria nearly a month already, but she hadn't ventured farther from Yosef and Miryam's new home than the nearest synagogue to the north of it, the nearest well to the south, nor the nearest market to the west.

Today, not long after Yosef read Abba's message to her, Dobah went for a walk while Levi napped. "Take as long as you want," Miryam had said to her, understanding in her eyes.

Dobah hadn't intended to go beyond the familiar, but her feet kept moving, and she allowed her mind to wander to her parents and to the dire news from Bethlehem. She recalled the night the soldiers had come. She remembered her quick goodbye to her abba on the outskirts of the village and the frightening race into the darkness with Menes. Menes. There seemed to be countless memories of him, of the ways he had protected her and Levi, of the smile that curved the corners of his mouth, of the sparkle in his dark eyes whenever he laughed. How she missed him. How she wished for his return.

When Dobah finally became aware of her surroundings again, she no longer knew where she was. Everything looked strange, and she feared she had left the Jewish quarter behind a long while before. She lifted her gaze above the nearest buildings and caught sight of an enormous structure beyond them. Several enormous structures.

"The Museum of Alexandria," she whispered, certain she was right.

Menes had told her about the complex that housed the great Alexandria library, as well as columned walkways, gardens, lecture halls, dining rooms, and meeting spaces where scholars from many nations gathered. Very near the library, although not where she could see at the moment, were the royal palaces and government administration buildings. And scattered nearby were the temples and altars to idols such as Serapis, Isis, and Horus.

Dobah remembered the temple of Serapis as they'd passed it on the day they arrived in Alexandria, and the memory made her shiver. She turned to hurry back the way she'd come. Or at least she hoped it was the way she'd come. Aware now of voices speaking foreign languages, she quickened her steps. She kept her eyes downcast, not wanting to meet the gazes of others, especially not the men who walked along the same street or talked in doorways.

Only after she saw a mezuzah on a doorpost did her breathing return to normal. The Jewish quarter was enormous, but at least she could ask questions of other women she met along the way, Jewish women who would help her find her way to the shop of Yosef ben Yakov, the tekton from Israel.

When at last she saw the familiar well, the one where she filled a water jar every morning, she had to fight not to break into a run. Tears of relief sprang to her eyes, and her heart pounded in her chest, so hard she wondered if others heard it too. Moments later she looked ahead and saw Yosef step through the doorway of his shop. Concern marked his face as he turned in her direction. The instant he saw her, his expression changed, his relief matching her own.

With long strides, he moved toward her. "Miryam has been beside herself." He pulled Dobah into an embrace. "And your son wants his imma."

"I am sorry I caused worry. I…I walked too far and lost my way."

He turned and guided her toward the shop entrance, his arm still around her shoulders. "This is not Bethlehem."

"I know that well enough."

Once inside the shop, Yosef called, "She is here, Miryam."

Hearing Levi's cries, Dobah broke away from her cousin and hurried through the workroom and up the stairs. She found Miryam walking the floor, Levi in her arms, bouncing him in an attempt to bring comfort.

When her son saw her, he held out both arms in Dobah's direction, nearly throwing himself out of Miryam's embrace. Dobah took him, holding him tight and kissing the top of his head. "I am sorry I was gone so long, Levi. I am sorry. I am here now."

"I would not do," Miryam said. "He wanted only you."

"I am sorry," Dobah said again, this time to Miryam. She went to a chair and sat on it. In moments, Levi's cries were silenced, replaced by slurping sounds as he nursed.

Dobah leaned close to his ear and whispered, "I will not wander that far from you ever again."

CHAPTER SEVENTEEN

It was cool and rainy on the day Menes finally returned to Yosef's shop. Yosef himself was away on a building project, and it was Miryam who called for Dobah. Hopeful for another message from her abba, she hurried down the stairs, Levi in her arms. When she saw Menes standing near the shop entrance, his dark hair and cloak wet from the rain, she came to an abrupt halt.

Over two months had passed since Levi had seen Menes, but the passage of time had not dimmed the little boy's memory. "Mens!" he squealed.

Menes grinned in response. "Shalom, Levi."

Dobah released the wriggling toddler, and he hurried toward Menes, giggles trailing behind him.

Like her son, Dobah wanted to laugh with glee. She had tried to tell herself she'd been wrong about her feelings for this man. She'd tried to tell herself it wouldn't matter to her if she never saw Menes again. Lies. They'd been lies. She wasn't wrong about how she felt, and she would have been devastated if he'd never returned to see her.

"You look well, Dobah," he said, his voice low, his eyes on her even as Levi tugged on his cloak.

She felt her cheeks grow warm. "As do you, Menes."

"I was hoping to speak with Yosef."

"He is working."

A smile tweaked the corners of his mouth. "So Miryam told me."

"Come in and sit." Dobah motioned toward a stool near the clay stove, a fire burning within to take the chill from the morning. "Warm yourself."

He lifted Levi into his arms—how right her son looked there—and walked to the stool.

"Have you been away?" Dobah asked. "Did you lead a caravan somewhere?"

"No. I have remained in Alexandria."

The answer caused a painful twinge in her heart. He'd been in the city, but he hadn't come to see her. Why?

"I have been studying," he added as he settled onto the stool.

Confused by the comment, she gave her head a small shake. "Studying?"

"Yes. I am studying with a teacher so I might join the Israelite community and follow Adonai's laws and customs."

"You want to become a *ger tzedek*?" Her heart skittered.

"Yes." His smile faded, and his expression was filled with determination. "That is my desire."

Dobah turned toward Miryam, who stood in the connecting doorway to the workroom. "Does Yosef know?"

Miryam gave a slight shrug.

"Dobah." Menes said her name softly, drawing her gaze back to him. "Yosef knew that was my stated intent. He did not know if I would persevere. But I have and I will."

"Why?" she whispered.

"Because Adonai is the Living God. This I knew before we left Bethlehem. But it is also because I want to take you as my wife. I must be a righteous convert in the eyes of your family and this community before that can happen."

"You want to marry me?" She sank onto a second stool, her legs suddenly too weak to hold her.

"I do."

"Yosef will agree? Or must we wait for you to ask Abba?"

"I believe Yosef is able to speak for your abba and that he will agree to the marriage. But not yet."

"Then when?"

"My Torah teacher is pleased with the progress I have made, but there is still much for me to know before I can be circumcised and immersed in the *mikveh*. Those first weeks I was like the younger children attending the Beth Sefer—only much taller." He smiled at his own attempt at humor.

Dobah looked down at her hands, clenched in her lap, even as her heart soared over his determination to become one with her people. She knew Abba had seen something in Menes for the short while the two men were together in Bethlehem. Enough so that he had entrusted Dobah and Levi into Menes's care on the night the soldiers came to the village. Perhaps Abba had known, even before Menes had known himself, what would happen in Alexandria.

"The teacher says my ability to memorize is excellent." His smile widened. "I have caught up with the boys in the Beth Talmud."

Levi slid off Menes's lap. Keeping a hand on Menes's knee, Levi took a step toward his imma and placed his other hand on her knee.

Dobah felt the connection flowing through her son, binding them together, making them a family.

Hurry, she wanted to say. *Finish your studies, Menes. Do it soon.*

At that moment, looking into Dobah's eyes, Menes wished to be a poet. Surely a poet could have described the feelings that made him go all soft on the inside.

For most of his life, Menes had lived among men. While he had hoped to marry one day, his experiences with women had been few. Certainly not of the kind that engaged a man's heart. He hadn't been sure he even knew what love was...until now.

Miryam cleared her throat, and only then did Menes realize how far forward he had leaned, how he'd instinctively wanted to draw closer to Dobah. As he pulled back, he cleared his own throat. "Levi has grown since I saw him last."

"Yes."

"And you. Do you feel at home in Alexandria now?"

"No. It is too big. Too many people." She glanced toward Miryam then back at Menes. "Too many temples that worship idols."

"That is true," he said softly.

"A month ago, I went for a walk. I was not paying attention, and I went outside the Jewish quarter. I became quite frightened before I found my way back."

Although she'd said getting lost had happened weeks ago, he saw the lingering fear in her eyes. It reminded him of those days after they'd fled Bethlehem, how often she had looked behind her, as if wondering if disaster hid in shadows. He wanted to draw her into his arms and assure her that he would keep her safe, but he knew that would be frowned upon by Miryam. They were not betrothed and wouldn't be for some time to come.

"We received a message from Abba," Dobah added, her voice cracking. "That same day. It is why I went for a long walk. Because of the news from Bethlehem."

He nodded, his chest suddenly tight.

"You know of it? You know what happened that night after we ran away?"

"Yes," he answered. "Word reached the synagogue where I study."

She lowered her gaze. "You and I heard what the soldiers were doing. We heard the cries. It is why we ran. It is why Abba sent Levi and me away with you. But I never fully grasped what happened that night until I learned Levi alone survived of all the boys his age." She wiped her eyes with her fingertips. "I knew those other little boys, those babies. I know their parents."

"'But my eyes are fixed on you, Sovereign Lord.'" The words he'd memorized only a few days before came softly at first then grew stronger and surer. "'In you I take refuge—do not give me over to death. Keep me safe from the traps set by evildoers, from the snares they have laid for me. Let the wicked fall into their own nets, while I pass by in safety.'"

She smiled a little, but it was the saddest smile he'd ever seen. He thought it might break his heart to look at her.

"Only Adonai knows why Levi was saved that night," Menes said. "Perhaps because he is related to the promised Messiah."

She nodded, and the two of them fell into silence.

CHAPTER EIGHTEEN

Six months later, in the month of Kislev, 4 BC

On the day of the ceremony marking Menes's formal acceptance into the Jewish community in Alexandria, a pleasant breeze wafted through the streets, bringing the promise of the cool rainy season. To Dobah, it seemed a blessing from Adonai, a sign of His good pleasure.

As the ceremony began, Dobah sat with Miryam and the other women in the synagogue, her heart filled with joy. Although Menes had completed the steps of his conversion to Judaism faster than many, the waiting had still seemed long to Dobah. But after today, they could begin planning their wedding and their future as a family. And they would do so with her abba's blessing as well as Yosef's approval.

When Chizkiyahu, the rabbi who had shepherded Menes during these past months, rose from his chair, Dobah's breath caught in her throat. The moment had come at last when Menes would receive his Hebrew name, a name symbolizing his new identity among her people. With one arm around her son, seated quietly on her lap, seeming to be as caught up by the ceremony as the adults around him, she reached with her free hand to take hold of Miryam's. She could hardly say why she felt suddenly nervous. Perhaps because she would call her husband by this new name for as long as they both lived.

A few words from the rabbi were lost in the jumble of her thoughts, but when he called Menes by his new name, she heard it as clear as anything.

"Ethan," she echoed softly, the name making her feel warm and joyful. Ethan meant strong, solid, enduring. If ever a name befit its bearer, such was true of the name chosen for her intended. He was all of those things. He was firm. He was safe.

Menes...no, Ethan...looked in her direction, his gaze capturing hers. Perhaps he understood the significance of his new name as much as she did, for he seemed to stand a little taller in that moment.

Adonai's ways were, indeed, mysterious. Her thoughts were not His thoughts and her ways not His ways. She could never have imagined herself sitting in a synagogue in Egypt, knowing she would marry a former gentile who had converted to Judaism.

A celebration followed the end of the ceremony. The tables in the courtyard were laden with an abundance of food provided by families in the synagogue. Grilled fish. Roasted lamb, seasoned with herbs and spices. An array of vegetables flavored with garlic, onions, and coriander. Honey cakes and many kinds of pastries and fruit dishes. The wine flowed freely. Musicians took up their instruments, and soon dancing began, men on one side of the courtyard and women on the other.

In the midst of the music, noise, and laughter, Levi slipped away from Dobah, moving so much faster now that he was two years old. She might have found it difficult to catch him in the crowd of revelers, but Ethan—oh, how she liked that new name—saw him first and scooped the little boy into his arms. Whispering in Levi's ear, he carried him toward Dobah.

"It is a great day," Ethan said after stopping before her.

"A great day."

"But Levi does not want to stay with his imma. He wants to run and dance with the others."

She glanced around the courtyard. "He is too young to remember the last wedding celebration we attended in Bethlehem." As happened so often, thoughts of the village where she'd lived all but the past nine months of her life brought a wave of homesickness with them. She shook her head to drive away the longing for home. This was not a day to be sad. This was a day to rejoice.

But Ethan must have noticed the change in her, no matter how brief. "Is something wrong?"

"No."

"You would rather be in Bethlehem."

She met his gaze. "Yes."

"Remember Yosef's dream. Remember what the angel of the Lord told him. He was to take Yeshua and Miryam and flee to Egypt. He was to remain in Egypt until…" He let the words hang in the air, waiting for her to finish them.

With a nod, she said, "Until the angel of the Lord tells him to return to Israel."

Ethan leaned his head closer to Dobah, tenderness in his dark eyes. "We are not in Egypt forever. This is for a time. That is all. Adonai knows when it will be safe, and we will go with Yosef and Miryam whenever they leave Alexandria. I believe in my heart that is what Adonai would have us do. Our place is with them."

His words eased Dobah's homesickness. She would try not to be impatient. Life in Alexandria was not terrible. Not here in the Jewish quarter of the city. She was comfortable living with her cousin and his family. She had made friends at the synagogue they attended. Levi was healthy and happy. She already loved the man she was soon to marry.

You have blessed us, Adonai, and I thank You.

Ethan passed Levi into her waiting arms, and there was something in his expression telling her he was grateful for Adonai's blessings as well.

After Ethan returned to the dancing, Dobah carried her son to a bench in the shade and sat on it. She was soon joined by Miryam. Yeshua struggled in his imma's grasp, demanding to be set on the ground. Not yet a year old, He had recently taken His first independent steps, and now He wanted to try to walk everywhere.

He is the long-awaited Messiah. But He seems no different than any other baby.

Dobah recalled the day she'd sat with Miryam on the rooftop and heard the story of Yeshua's miraculous conception. She believed and still she wondered how it could be true. "So strange," she said beneath her breath.

Miryam looked at her, a question in her eyes.

Dobah gave a small shake of her head. She didn't want to try to explain her thoughts. And yet, wasn't she right? Wasn't it strange she could believe Yeshua was who others said He was and yet wonder at it, all at the same time? He was such an ordinary little boy. He looked a great deal like Levi had a year ago—olive skin, pudgy legs, adorable little feet, curly dark hair, large brown eyes, and a grin that showed His baby teeth.

A burst of laughter came from a group of men standing off to the courtyard's right side. Both Dobah and Miryam looked in that direction. Dobah found her cousin in the midst of them, motioning with his hands.

Miryam said, "He is describing the project he and Menes...I mean, Ethan...are working on."

"How do you know?"

"Because he has described it to me and used those exact same gestures and worn that exact same expression." She laughed softly.

"You sound like Imma. She can tell what Abba is thinking without him saying a word."

"Mmm." Miryam continued to smile as she watched Yosef.

"It was never like that for me with Dover. He was a mystery to me in many ways. I could rarely guess what he was thinking, even though I knew him almost my entire life."

Miryam turned toward her again.

"He was a good husband," Dobah rushed to say, "but it was not the same between us as it is with you and Yosef." What she wanted to say was that there had been no passion between them. Their love had been the type that came from long acquaintance. But Dover had never teased her the way she'd seen Abba tease Imma. Dover had never drawn her suddenly into an embrace the way she'd seen Yosef pull Miryam close before kissing her when he thought no one was looking.

With her eyes, she sought out Ethan. He had left the group of dancers and now stood alone near a table, a goblet in hand. Love welled within her as she looked at him. Undeniable love. Strong and sure love. Strong and sure like Ethan, who had once been Menes.

One day, in the not-too-distant future, she believed she would see him talking with a group of men, and she would know the story he told them simply because she knew him in her heart. Because she had lived with him and slept with him and eaten with him.

"Yosef will not make you wait long," Miryam said.

Dobah turned to her dear friend. "Is it so obvious?"

"Your impatience?" Miryam laughed again. "Yes."

Heat rose in Dobah's cheeks, but she could not deny the truth. She was impatient to become Ethan's wife and to begin their new life together.

Dobah married Ethan one month later, on a day without wind or rain. The sky was a clear blue, and a pleasant warmth blanketed Alexandria, a blessing from on high. Friends from the synagogue joined in the celebration of the union, but Dobah still noticed all those who were missing—her parents and grandmother, the neighbors she had known her entire life, girls she had studied with in the synagogue, memorizing the *Shema* and other words from the Torah before they left school to learn how to be good wives. Oh, how she wished she and Ethan could have been with them in Bethlehem. How she wished to share the joy that had come to her after many sorrows.

Dobah had not been quite fifteen when she and Dover married. After the wedding celebration, they had moved into the room Dover had added to his abba's house. She had lived there with her husband for more than two years. But then Dover's imma had fallen ill and died. Little more than a week later, Dover had died in a terrible accident, killed beneath a wagon that lost its wheel, and Dobah had returned to her parents' home to mourn and await the birth of her son.

Now she was past twenty, and Levi was two. They lived in a huge city far from Israel, far from the village that had been home to them. As newlyweds, she and Ethan would not move into a family home. They would have their own small household, one block away from Yosef's shop.

"You are happy, my wife?" Ethan whispered near her ear.

A shiver ran up her spine as his breath caressed the skin of her neck. "I am."

"It is my wish you will always be happy."

"I do not believe such a thing is possible. To always be happy. We have both known grief in this life. We will know it again."

His smile was tender. "Perhaps. But as far as it is in my power to make you happy, Dobah, I will do so."

She believed him, and she promised in her heart she would do the same for him.

Much like the day when Ethan had been accepted into the Jewish community, the tables were laden with food and the wine flowed freely. Darkness fell early in this season, and soon a black sky formed a canopy over the merrymaking. Oil lamps flickered on tables. Laughter and music filled the night air.

Dobah was talking to Miryam and Yosef when Ethan came to stand beside her. Without a word, she knew he had come to take her to their new home.

Smiling gently, Miryam said, "Levi will see you in the morning."

And with that, Dobah and Ethan slipped away into the night.

CHAPTER NINETEEN

While young children played in the middle of the communal washing area, their mothers and sisters—Dobah and Miryam among them—labored over basins filled with water, scrubbing clothes with soap made from ash and plant oils. Multiple conversations swirled around Dobah, but she paid attention to none of them. Her thoughts were on her husband.

On their wedding day, she'd told him it wasn't possible for a person to be happy all the time. Now she wasn't so sure. She awakened with happiness overflowing in her heart and a smile on her lips. She cooked food with a smile. She swept the floor with a smile. She went to the market with a smile. She even washed clothes with a smile. She was happy, through and through, and Ethan had made her that way. Adonai had blessed her and given her joy in this new marriage.

Keep him safe, Adonai. Grant him Your favor. May he know You more and more.

Children's laughter drew her gaze to where Levi sat with Yeshua, circled by other children of various ages. Levi and Yeshua could have been brothers, they looked so much alike. She hoped they would love each other as brothers too. But she also hoped she and Ethan would have more children, that Adonai would fill their quiver with sons and daughters.

An elbow nudged Dobah's arm, and she turned her head to look at Avigail. The woman—perhaps a couple of years older than Dobah—lived nearby, and they attended the same synagogue. She was the mother of three daughters with another child expected in a few months.

"Do you have news to share?" Avigail asked.

"News?"

"It is the way you were smiling. As if you have a secret." Avigail leaned closer. "Perhaps you are with child?"

Dobah shook her head. "We have been married less than two weeks."

"For some of us that hardly matters." Avigail placed a hand on her rounded belly.

In her first marriage, Dobah had waited more than two years before she became pregnant. How she'd thanked Adonai when she'd learned she wasn't barren, a fear that had taken hold in her heart.

Avigail seemed about to say something more but sounds from near the well drew her attention away from Dobah to where two women were talking. One gestured with excitement as she spoke. Another woman joined them, and then another. Soon the news began to spread throughout the communal washing area.

It was Miryam who told the news to Dobah. "King Herod is dead."

The feared king, the man who had wanted to kill Yeshua and had murdered little children in his effort to succeed, was dead himself.

"Is Yeshua safe now?" Dobah asked in a hushed voice, not wanting anyone else to hear, not even Avigail who was currently talking to the woman on her other side.

"I do not know." Miryam shook her head. "Herod commanded that upon his death recently imprisoned Jewish elders were to be killed. It is said he wanted to ensure that Israel would mourn and no one would have mourned Herod's death itself. Others had to die for true mourning to take place."

Dobah covered her mouth. There had been no end to the evil of Herod, and yet the news of his last wishes still surprised and horrified her.

Miryam placed her fingertips on the back of Dobah's wrist. "Yosef will know more when he returns from the building site. I am sure of it. Take supper with us tonight, and we will hear what our husbands have to tell us."

Dobah nodded her compliance even as her thoughts churned. Who would reign over Israel in Herod's place? Would it be one of his sons, and if so, were they as evil as Herod himself? Were they also afraid that the promised Messiah had been born in Bethlehem? Had any of them been present when the magi met with the king? Might Rome decide to govern Israel in a different way?

She closed her eyes. *O for the day to come when Israel will be rid of its oppressors!*

Her gaze returned to Yeshua, seated on the stone paving beside Levi. Was He truly the king who would lead His people to freedom? The son of a tekton and an ordinary girl from Nazareth. A baby born in a stable in Bethlehem. Could this toddler truly grow up to be a warrior-king who would lead other men against the Roman Empire, setting Israel free?

There she was again, believing and unbelieving at the same time. How she wished her belief was more steadfast and sure. Like

Ethan's. He never seemed to waver. From the moment he'd bowed along with the magi, he'd been certain of who Yeshua was, and his trust in Adonai had only grown as he'd studied the Torah and the prophets and read the Book of Praises, memorizing many of them in the months since they'd arrived in Alexandria.

As she returned to scrubbing the clothing in the basin, words from one of the songs of ascent filled her heart.

"I lift up my eyes to the mountains—where does my help come from? My help comes from the Lord, the Maker of heaven and earth."

In her memory, she heard Abba's and Imma's voices singing the words. She pictured herself as a little girl, her sisters holding her hands as they walked up the road to Jerusalem to celebrate the festival.

"He will not let your foot to slip—He who watches over you will not slumber; indeed He who watches over Israel will neither slumber nor sleep. The Lord watches over you—the Lord is your shade at your right hand."

It was true. Adonai had kept her. He never slumbered. He was the shade on her right hand.

"The sun will not harm you by day, nor the moon by night. The Lord will keep you from all harm—He will watch over your life; the Lord will watch over your coming and going both now and forevermore."

"I will not doubt," she whispered. "I will *not* doubt."

The men returned from their labors as dusk settled over the earth. The air had turned chilly during the afternoon, clouds blocking out the sun, and both Yosef and Ethan were thankful for the fire that not only cooked their supper but could warm them as well.

Miryam did not wait long to ask questions about the news that had spread through the Jewish quarter earlier in the day. Sadly, there were few additional details. Herod was dead, and it was believed one of his surviving sons would take the throne.

"Do you think it is true, what they are saying about the Jewish elders?" Dobah asked. "That he demanded them killed after his death."

Yosef's expression was grim. "There is no reason not to believe it. He murdered three of his own sons. He murdered the children of Bethlehem. Why not our elders?"

Dobah's breath caught in her chest. It was as if she felt the pursuit of Herod's soldiers once again. No one spoke for a long while, each lost in their own thoughts.

Levi rose from where he'd been playing with small blocks of wood, stacking one upon another then waiting as Yeshua knocked them over with a sweep of a pudgy hand. Her son came to stand before Ethan and raised his arms in a silent demand to be picked up. Ethan complied with a smile.

"How is our boy today?" her husband asked as he pressed his forehead against Levi's.

Levi responded by patting Ethan's cheeks and giggling.

The image of the two of them blurred as tears welled in Dobah's eyes. Adonai had not only given her a loving husband, but He had given Levi an abba too. Adonai's mercies never failed. Even a wicked king like Herod could not obscure that truth.

After blinking away the tears, her gaze shifted to Yosef, who now held Yeshua in his arms. Looking at them, it occurred to her neither of these men were the natural father of the sons they held. These boys had been born to their wives but sired by another.

Levi by Dover ben Natan.

Yeshua by the Ruach HaKodesh.

Five days later, Ethan awakened in the morning with a strange feeling stirring in his soul. It wasn't anything he could describe. It wasn't fear or dread. It wasn't worry. It was more a sense that something was about to change.

He sat on the side of the bed, closed his eyes, and placed his hands on his knees, palms up. Whispering, he prayed, "I offer thanks to You, living and eternal King, for You have mercifully restored my soul within me. Your faithfulness is great."

Behind him on the bed, Dobah stirred. She would be fully awake soon, and he wanted to have a fire made before she got out of bed. The cool, damp weather had clung to Alexandria for days, making these first hours of the morning uncomfortable until a fire chased the chill from their small apartment.

A short while later, with Dobah preparing a meal to break their fast and Ethan readying for another workday, a knock sounded at their door, surprising them both. The last person he expected to find when he opened the door was Yosef.

"Am I late?" Ethan asked, glancing out at the sky.

"No." Yosef shook his head, his expression solemn. "I have had another dream."

Ethan held the door open wide, and Yosef entered the room.

Dobah came to stand beside Ethan, taking hold of his arm. "The angel of the Lord has come to you again?"

"Yes." Yosef's gaze moved back and forth between the two of them. "He said, 'Get up, take the child and his mother and go to the land of Israel, for those who were trying to take the child's life are dead.'"

Ethan nodded. "How soon will we leave?"

"As quickly as possible. I feel an urgency to obey."

"We will be ready."

"Our job in the city will be finished by tonight. Tomorrow, we will buy a donkey and cart to carry what we will take back with us to Israel."

"And the sale of your shop and home?"

"I will let others at the synagogue know it is for sale, and it will be according to Adonai's will. He will provide."

Ethan nodded again.

Yosef opened the door. "We will leave for the worksite when you are ready. Meet me at the shop."

"I will be ready soon. I only need time to eat."

With a nod, Yosef left.

"We are going home," Dobah said, sounding breathless.

It didn't surprise Ethan that he felt the same anticipation. For nearly two decades, he had been a wanderer, a boy and then a man without a home. He had traveled to many lands, had seen many nations. He had returned to Egypt. But it had never felt like home. It was the land of his birth, but Israel was now his home.

"Yes," he answered at last. "We are going home."

CHAPTER TWENTY

On the day of their departure, Dobah walked with Ethan, Yosef, and Miryam, the two little boys riding in the cart, through Alexandria. In many ways, the day was similar to the one when Dobah, Ethan, and Levi arrived in the city a little over nine and a half months earlier. The opulence and decadence of the city hadn't changed. But today was different too. Different because last time they'd been running away from danger. Different because this time they were headed home.

As they moved through the morning shadows cast onto the street by the temple of Serapis, words from a song of David drifted into her mind. *"From His temple He heard my voice."*

She smiled. In about a month, she would be in the land of her birth. She would be away from Egypt and the abundance of false gods. She would be in Israel where her people worshiped the Living God.

High-pitched giggles from the cart drew her gaze to the boys. They were too young to remember their journeys to Egypt. They weren't worried about the weeks of travel, about the weather, about food and water, about bandits and Roman soldiers, about the reduced number of coins in their purses. Levi and Yeshua weren't concerned about tomorrow or the days and weeks that would follow it, and their childish trust brought another song to her mind. *"I keep my eyes always on the Lord. With Him at my right hand, I will not be shaken."*

Her gaze went to Ethan, where he was leading the donkey that pulled the cart, Yosef walking on the other side of the animal. The placement of the two men caused people to make way for the cart in the crowded street. But soon they would leave the bustling seaport city of Alexandria behind them. Soon the sights and sounds would change. Instead of voices speaking in different languages, she would hear the creak of the cart wheels as they rolled along a dusty road.

Ethan will guide us safely home, just as he brought us safely here.

"What are you thinking?" Miryam asked.

Dobah hardly knew how to answer her friend. Her thoughts had flitted from one thing to another since the small party left Yosef's workshop and their home in the Jewish quarter, the new owner holding the key to the front door. And from what Ethan had told her, the new owner had taken advantage of Yosef's desire to leave as quickly as possible.

Miryam touched Dobah's arm. "The riches were never ours. Adonai has provided as He sees fit."

Had Miryam read her mind? "Ethan said the man cheated Yosef."

"Do you think any of this took Adonai by surprise?"

Dobah shook her head. "You are younger than me, Miryam, and yet I always seem to be learning from you. Still, it does not seem fair that Yosef should lose money on the transaction."

"My family has always been poor, Dobah. Yosef has great skills that he learned from his abba, but his family is not wealthy either. The men work hard and they provide for their loved ones, and that is enough. Through the gifts of the magi, Adonai made a way for us to come to Egypt without being destitute or afraid. Out of His benevolence, He gave us a place to live. He provided work for Yosef to do while we were in exile. Now we are going home, and Adonai will provide once again, in whatever way He chooses."

"'I keep my eyes always on the Lord,'" Dobah recited. "'With Him at my right hand, I will not be shaken.'"

Miryam gave her a querying glance.

"You are never shaken," she answered.

Her friend released a laugh. "Oh, Dobah. That is not true. I am shaken at times. More often than I care to admit. But then I remember El Shaddai and set Him before me again, just as we are told to do." Her gaze went to the young boys in the cart. "Sometimes, I lie awake in the dark, wondering what it means to be the imma of the Messiah. How will I not fail Him? I know so little. When will I see in Him what others will one day see? All I see now is my son, my baby boy who I need to feed and change and wash. Will I be blind to what others see, or will I know?"

"I did not know you wondered such things."

"Why would you? But I wonder. Yosef wonders too. Why were we chosen to be His parents, out of all the men and women of Israel? What will we have to teach Him?"

"He is only a year old. You do not need to teach Him much."

Miryam's smile was wistful. "Not now. But one day."

Dobah found herself suddenly thankful that Levi was an ordinary boy. She would teach him to pray the Shema. She would tell him the stories of their people found in the Torah. She would discipline him when he needed disciplined, and she would bandage his injuries when he fell and hurt himself. When he was older, he would attend Beth Sefer and Beth Talmud in the local synagogue. If he excelled in his studies of the *Tanakh*, perhaps he would find a master and become one of that rabbi's *talmidim*. He would learn his abba's trade. He would go to Jerusalem for the festivals. He would marry under a *chuppah* and bring his bride home to his abba's house. He would become an abba himself, and she would rock her grandchildren to sleep.

"Dobah, your thoughts have wandered far away again."

She smiled as she looked toward Miryam. "You have given me much to think about, my dear cousin. Much to think about."

"I have grown soft," Ethan told Yosef as the men made camp for the night.

They had covered a lot of ground this first day of travel, enough that Alexandria had long since been lost from sight. But not as far as he'd once traveled with the caravans. He'd walked greater distances in a day and given it little thought. Not so today. He was tired and ready to rest.

Their supper was simple fare, and as night settled over the earth, each young family retired to their tents with words of blessing, one to the other.

As tired as Ethan was, sleep did not come quickly, not even with Dobah nestled against his side. He remembered the journey with the magi that had taken him to Bethlehem. He recalled the past months in Alexandria. He imagined the future before them in Israel.

"You cannot sleep," Dobah said softly.

"Mmm."

"What troubles you?"

"I am not troubled, my love, but my thoughts will not settle."

She released a soft sigh that spread warmth across his skin. "I am the same."

He rolled onto his side and drew her closer, resting his cheek against the crown of her head. "Did you imagine, when we made our way to Egypt and others mistook us for husband and wife, that it would one day be true?"

"I *wanted* to imagine it, even when it seemed impossible. I loved you before my mind understood what my heart felt."

He moved his mouth close to her ear and whispered, "'A wife of noble character who can find? She is worth far more than rubies. Her husband has full confidence in her and lacks nothing of value. She brings him good, not harm, all the days of her life.'" He took a breath then added, "King Lemuel was a wise man."

"Is that how you see me?"

"I see you that way because it is true, Dobah. You are good, and you do good. And as surely as Adonai sent the star to bring the magi to Bethlehem, so I believe He wanted me to find you. He willed for us to be together, you and I." He kissed her temple.

She was silent a long while, and he thought she'd fallen asleep. Then she said, "You must promise me to always be careful, Ethan."

"Careful?"

"Never stand too near a heavy wagon that could fall on you. I want us to grow old together. I could not bear to lose you."

He understood then, and his heart broke a little for the pain of Dobah's past. "I will be as careful as I am able, my love. I promise."

CHAPTER TWENTY-ONE

On the third morning of their journey, they met another family of four headed for Israel. They were Zissa and her husband, Kalman; their granddaughter, Frema; and Frema's husband, Tobias. Upon first sight, Dobah was drawn to the elderly woman, perhaps because Zissa resembled Dobah's savta, from her tiny stature to her thinning gray hair to the deep crevices that lined her face to the translucent skin on the backs of her hands. Ethan was quick to offer Zissa a place in the donkey cart beside Levi and Yeshua, and there she stayed.

The next day other families fell in with them until their original group of six increased to a total of twenty-four—fifteen adults and nine children.

On this warm afternoon, a week later, as they followed the cart carrying the elderly woman and several children, Dobah looked at Zissa's granddaughter, who walked beside her. Frema seemed a very private sort of person, and she had interacted little with others outside of her own family, since their parties merged. Now, Frema's left hand was pressed against the center of her back while her right hand rested on the swell of her belly and a frown furrowed her brow.

Dobah broke the silence that accompanied them. "Perhaps you should take a turn in the cart. You look uncomfortable."

Frema shook her head. "It jostles too much. I am better off walking." It was the most Frema had said to Dobah all week.

Encouraged, Dobah asked, "How long before your child is born?"

"Perhaps two months."

"I hope it will go well with you."

"As do I. Tobias and I have prayed for this child for many years."

That comment surprised Dobah. She'd assumed Frema—older than Dobah by perhaps five or six years—was a newlywed since she and Tobias had no other children.

In answer to Dobah's unspoken question, Frema said, "This is not the first child I have conceived, but it is the first to remain in my womb this many months."

A lump of sympathy formed in Dobah's throat, and she could do nothing but nod.

Frema stared at the cart. "Your son is strong and healthy. How old is he?"

"Levi is three now."

"May Adonai bless you and keep you." Frema spoke softly, barely loud enough for Dobah to hear. "May Adonai's light shine upon you, and may He be gracious to you. May you feel Adonai's Presence within you always, and may you find peace."

At first Dobah thought the blessing was for Levi, since Frema was looking at him, but then she wondered if Frema meant the blessing for her unborn child.

"How long have you and Ethan been married?"

The question surprised her, more because Frema seemed to want to continue the conversation than anything else. "Not yet a full month."

"A month? But I thought…" She paused then said, "You have Levi."

"Levi's abba died before Levi was born. He was killed in an accident on the road outside of Bethlehem."

"I did not know. I am sorry."

"Adonai is gracious and merciful, even in heartache." She looked toward Ethan.

"Did you meet your husband in Alexandria?"

Two memories flashed in Dobah's mind in quick succession. The night Menes had led her away from Bethlehem, Levi in his arms, terrified screams following them into the darkness. And then the day he'd been accepted as a ger tzedek at the synagogue in Alexandria and received his new name.

"In a way," she said at last.

Perhaps Frema would have asked Dobah to explain her cryptic answer, but the cart in front of them stopped suddenly, causing them to do the same. Dobah's gaze found Ethan again. Something in his stance alarmed her and she moved toward the cart, ready to take Levi in her arms.

"What is it?" she heard one of the women behind her ask.

The men—seven of them, all but Zissa's husband who had stationed himself in front of the cart—had gathered ahead of the others, conversing in low voices. Dobah saw Ethan's hand touch his waist, as if to be certain his knife was there. That was the gesture that caused her heart to race.

They had left Egypt behind them and were following the coastal highway through Nabatene. The Nabateans were a fiercely independent people, still free of the rule of Rome, unlike their neighbors. That meant there were no Roman patrol units on this stretch of the highway.

Dobah looked beyond the men. Ahead of them, the road narrowed as it passed between two hills. The terrain was barren and still. She didn't know what had alarmed Ethan, but she trusted his instincts and took a step closer to Levi.

Suddenly, a guttural shout broke the late afternoon air. From the shadows, men leaped into view. They were ragged figures, brandishing crude weapons, their eyes alight with the prospect of easy plunder.

Ethan moved with a precision and agility that spoke of his years of experience as a khabir. He dodged the first bandit's clumsy swing, countering with a swift kick to the man's knee then a right hook to his jaw. The bandit crumpled to the ground with a cry of pain.

Dobah grabbed Levi from the cart and held him close against her body, ready to flee if it became necessary. From the corner of her eye, she saw the other mothers doing the same, youngest children in their arms, older children clinging to their mothers' cloaks.

Tobias, not a tall man but ruggedly built, caught one of the bandits in the arm with his knife, drawing blood. The bandit shouted in alarm as Tobias pursued him. Another bandit was knocked to the ground, his weapon sliding down the road to land in front of the donkey's hooves. Kalman picked it up. Although bent with age, the older man seemed ready to use the weapon should any thief approach the women and children.

Seeing they had underestimated the resolve of their intended victims, one of the bandits shouted. Then they all turned and disappeared into the lengthening shadows. Almost as quickly as it had begun, the skirmish was over.

"Is anyone hurt?" Ethan asked even as his gaze sought her out.

"We are all right," someone answered.

"I am fine," another said.

Others answered the same.

Ethan rubbed his right hand with his left as he moved toward Dobah.

Holding Levi on her hip, she met him halfway. With her free arm, she reached out to take his right hand. The knuckles were red and scraped. "We are good but you are not."

"That? It is nothing. Not even sure how it happened."

"I am. You punched the bandit who tried to club you."

Ethan grinned. He resembled a little boy who was pleased he'd just won a game of some kind.

Suddenly irritated, she demanded, "Do you think this is funny?"

"No. But we ran them off. That is what matters."

"You might have been seriously hurt. You might have been killed."

He put an arm around their shoulders, embracing both her and her son. His grin disappeared. "But I was not hurt, Dobah. I was not killed. And you and Levi are safe from harm. Adonai be praised."

Pressing her face against his chest, she echoed, "Adonai be praised."

That night, the men took extra care, standing guard two at a time in two-hour shifts.

Dobah awakened when Ethan rose to take his turn and remained awake until he returned to their tent. "How long until we are home again?" she whispered as he settled onto their bed of blankets, Levi asleep between them.

"Perhaps another fifteen days, if all goes well."

"Will I feel safer once I see Roman patrols again, or will I be even more afraid?"

It was an impossible question for Ethan to answer, and she knew it. So he drew her closer, sandwiching Levi in the warmth of their bodies. And at long last, Dobah fell back to sleep.

She dreamed she was alone in the streets of Bethlehem. She knew it was her village and yet it looked different. She was running and running, looking behind her, hearing screams. Panic iced her heart. Where was Levi? Where were Abba and Imma? Off to her right, a child cried out in alarm. Was it Levi? She tried to see, but it was too dark. There were no stars in the heavens, no moon, no lights in the windows of the houses. A hot wind, like an evil breath, brushed against the back of her neck. She wanted to add her own scream to those she heard, but she was unable to make a sound. Her feet felt like stones. Large stones that would drag her to the bottom if water came pouring down the street. Water or no water, it seemed she was drowning.

Help! her mind cried. *Adonai, have mercy!*

The scene changed abruptly. The night turned to day. The village turned to hillsides where sheep grazed upon tender shoots. And up ahead of her, she saw Ethan walking toward her with Levi riding on his shoulders.

Adonai is my Shepherd...Adonai is my Shepherd...Adonai is my Shepherd.

The dream faded away, and she slept peacefully until the dawn.

CHAPTER TWENTY-TWO

The weather turned colder, and it rained every day. Not heavy rain or for long periods but enough to make all the travelers wet and miserable. The distance the group covered in a day was shortened. Everyone was eager for a campfire to dry their clothes and warm their bones.

At the end of another day of rain and wind, Dobah squatted near the campfire, a pot of lentils beginning to bubble. "Miryam, we do not have enough food to feed us all for the rest of the journey."

"I know. Both the dried fish and fruit are nearly gone. But the men are hunting. Perhaps they will kill a gazelle. Yosef is certain he saw one running away from the cistern earlier."

The food supplies had seemed ample when their small party left Alexandria. But they hadn't anticipated joining forces with an elderly couple and their pregnant granddaughter and her husband. Those four had come from Memphis with only what they could carry. And so, Dobah and Miryam had shared from their own stores, all the while praying Adonai would provide what they needed.

Dobah stood. "If you watch the kettle, I will get more water."

Miryam nodded.

After grabbing another pot, Dobah made her way to the cistern, hidden near the base of a rocky hillside. The Nabataeans were known for their skill in managing scarce water resources, creating hidden water cisterns in the desert. Ethan knew of this one because of the years he'd traveled with caravans.

"Another way You have provided for us," she said softly. "My husband knows the trade routes."

After filling the pot with water, she stood and began her walk to the campground. A movement from the corner of her eye caused her to stop and turn. She saw a snake slithering across the dry earth in her direction and stepped back instinctively. The gravel beneath her sandals slid one way and her body shifted another. The pot fell to the ground, splashing her with water as she fell and began to slide down the hill on her left side. She cried out in a mixture of pain and alarm a moment before coming to an abrupt halt.

"Dobah!"

She opened her eyes to see Ethan through her tears. "There was a snake."

"Did it strike you?" He knelt beside her.

"No. It only startled me."

He helped her sit up, and the world seemed to roll and whirl. She closed her eyes against the sensation.

"You are bleeding," he said.

She opened her eyes again, looking first at the scrapes on her arm then the ones on her leg. "It is not bad." She drew a breath. "Were you successful?"

"What?"

"Did you kill a gazelle?"

He released a humorless chuckle. "No, we were not so fortunate as that."

"I am sorry."

"We were returning to camp when I saw you take that tumble." He grasped her more firmly and helped her to her feet.

The sting of her scrapes grew worse. Her skin felt taut, as if it were suddenly too small to encase her body. Her head swam.

"I do not—" she began. And then the world went black.

Ethan carried his unconscious wife into the campsite. As soon as they saw Dobah, Miryam, Zissa, and Frema leaped into action. All Ethan could do was place Dobah on a blanket and stand back while the women tended to her. Relief flooded through him when, not long after, Dobah moaned, moved her head, and finally opened her eyes.

"What happened?" she asked.

"You fainted," Miryam answered.

"Why would I faint? I am not that hurt."

Zissa, gently washing the blood from Dobah's left leg with a wet piece of cloth, said, "Hurt enough. Lie still and let us help you."

Dobah looked around until she found Ethan. He saw both confusion and frustration in her dark eyes. He agreed her injuries didn't seem to be serious enough to cause her to faint. But perhaps she'd sprained an ankle in the fall. That might explain it.

As if to test the theory, Miryam said, "Can you move your feet and hands?"

"Of course." Dobah did so, first swiveling one wrist then the other. Next one ankle then the other. She didn't grimace or cry out. "See. I am all right."

Without being asked, Miryam put an arm beneath Dobah's back and eased her into a sitting position.

"It was silly of me. I do not like snakes, but they do not make me faint. The only other time I have fainted was when—" Her words broke off abruptly. Her gaze shot to Ethan, her eyes gone wide.

He thought she looked as if she might faint a second time.

"Ethan." His name came out on a breath.

"What?" He took a step closer.

When she smiled, it was as if the clouds had parted and the sun shone through, but it left him even more alarmed than before. Miryam and the other two women stood and slipped away, as if ordered to do so. Ethan had the distinct feeling they understood something he had yet to grasp.

He knelt beside Dobah. "What?"

"It is good we are going home to Bethlehem."

"Of course."

"I will need my imma and sisters to be with me."

He nodded. He knew she missed them.

"I will want them to help deliver our baby."

The breath caught in his chest, and for a moment, he wondered if he might pass out too. The sound of her laughter brought him back from the brink.

"You are certain?" he asked.

"I had not realized it an hour ago. With traveling and the weather and all there was to think about, I did not consider the passage of time." Her smile returned. "But yes, I am certain."

"Your fall?"

She reached out and touched his cheek. "The child is fine. It was not such a hard fall."

"We should have stayed in Alexandria. If I had known—"

"Adonai knew."

His pulse quickened at her words, and he recalled words from a song of King David. *For You created my inmost being; You knit me together in my mother's womb.* "Yes, He knew. We will not be afraid."

"We will not be afraid," she echoed.

CHAPTER TWENTY-THREE

It was midday, and they were somewhere south of Gaza when Zissa, Kalman, Frema, and Tobias bid them a tearful farewell. Others who had traveled with them out of Egypt had gone their separate ways even before reaching the border of Israel. Now it would be only the six of them once again.

Zissa placed the flat of her wrinkled hand on Dobah's cheek. "You are filled with kindness. I do not know what would have become of us without your generosity. Yours and Miryam's and your husbands'."

"May Adonai go with you."

"And with you." With a watery smile, Zissa turned, took hold of her husband's arm, and walked away, Frema and Tobias following right behind.

After a lengthy silence, Dobah said, "We are almost home."

Ethan put an arm around her shoulders. "Perhaps three days."

His words echoed in her heart. Three days and she would stand in the circle of Abba's arms. Three days and she would bask in Imma's smile.

"Ethan," Yosef said. "Dobah."

They turned toward her cousin.

"You should know something. We will not go with you to Bethlehem."

"But Yosef—"

"Archelaus rules Judea in the place of his father. It is not safe for Yeshua there. Not now. Adonai has told me to take Him and His mother into Galilee. Once we reach Ashkelon, we will part ways with you. Miryam and I will go north to Nazareth, and you and Ethan will turn east on your way to Bethlehem."

"Yosef," Dobah whispered, her vision blurring. She hadn't considered that he and Miryam might not go to her village again. It shouldn't surprise her. They had come from Nazareth at the time of the census. It made sense they would return there now. Still...

"We will see each other again, Cousin." Yosef glanced at Yeshua and Levi in the back of the cart. "And our boys will be together at the time of the festivals as they grow older."

She knew what he said was true. Yosef had never been one to miss the festivals in Jerusalem. Every Pesach, every Shavuot, every Sukkot, he had made the journey to the holy city along with other pilgrims from Galilee, as commanded in the law. Only their time in Egypt had kept him away. Still, her heart ached.

"We will come to Jerusalem for Pesach. That is less than two months from now."

Dobah drew in a slow, deep breath. Yosef was right. It was not so very long until Pesach. Still, it would be strange, not sitting with Miryam in the synagogue, not watching Yeshua and Levi play, not sharing a meal.

Yosef grinned. "And we are not to Ashkelon yet, so do not begin missing us already."

She laughed, although she didn't feel merry.

Ethan squeezed her shoulders then released her. "Come. We want to cover much ground before we make camp for the night."

Star of Wonder: Dobah's Story

That night, Dobah lay on the mat and stared up at the stars through the opening in the tent flap. Levi lay snug against her side, seeking her warmth, and behind him was Ethan, snoring softly.

Home. She was almost home. But she wasn't the same woman who had fled with her child into the night. She had changed. Had Abba and Imma? Were they well? She had received only two messages from Bethlehem during her exile in Alexandria, and her abba would never have wasted precious words about his health.

She placed her hands on her abdomen. Her stomach was flat, giving no hint of the child growing within. A blessing from Adonai. Perhaps another son to work beside his abba. Or perhaps this time she would give birth to a daughter.

A star shot across the heavens, a white tail in its wake. A life could be like that. There for a moment, and then darkened. Gone forever. Only Adonai knew what tomorrow would bring.

Would Ethan be content in Bethlehem? Would he work for her abba, as he'd done for a short time before the coming of the soldiers? He had loved working with Yosef, but Yosef would be in Nazareth and Ethan would be in Bethlehem. Most men learned their trade as boys. Ethan's trade had been leading great caravans. Would he want to return to that work? Would he regret marrying her with time? No, he wouldn't. He loved her, of that she was certain. Still, the unknowns crowded in, worrying her.

One of Ethan's hands covered both of hers on her abdomen. "You are not sleeping again." His voice was soft but gravelly.

"I have many thoughts going through my head."

"'She is clothed in strength and dignity; she can laugh at the days to come.'" He drew closer, sandwiching Levi between them. "'She speaks with wisdom, and faithful instruction is on her tongue.'" He kissed her ear then whispered, "Those words describe you, my love."

"I do not always smile at the future."

"You do, and you do it with strength and dignity."

"You are too generous, my husband."

He nuzzled her neck. "Only honest."

She rolled her head to the side and kissed his crown. "They will leave us tomorrow."

"Yes."

"I am going to miss them."

"Adonai will be with them, as He is with us."

"I know." She closed her eyes. "I wonder so often when it will be clear to others who Yeshua is. He seems so much like Levi, I cannot always believe it is true."

"It is true."

"The Messiah, growing up the son of a tekton in Nazareth. Will anyone believe it?"

"I have much yet to learn from the Scriptures, Dobah. I am new to the faith. But this I know. Adonai calls us out of places and sets us on a path we would never have chosen or imagined. Will it be so different, even for the Messiah?"

"I do not know."

He kissed her. "Then we must wait and see together." As he spoke, he rolled onto his back, one arm across his forehead.

"Wait and see." She laid her head on his shoulder. "We will wait and see."

CHAPTER TWENTY-FOUR

While Dobah was able to see the golden gleam of Herod's Temple from afar, her little village nestled in the Judean hills to the south of Jerusalem wasn't as clear to her until she got much closer to its familiar streets and buildings. And with each step she took on the road leading her home, her heart pounded harder in her chest.

"Go, Dobah. Run ahead. Levi and I will not be far behind."

She sent Ethan a grateful look before breaking into a run, not caring how she must appear. She ran past sheep on a hillside, past women washing clothes in a stream. She left the road to follow a familiar path toward the family vineyard, not needing to decide where to go first, her feet deciding for her. She recognized her abba, standing between rows of grapevines, which were brown and gnarled in this season. He wore his most colorful cloak. As if he'd known she would be coming today and would need to see him from a distance.

"Abba! Abba!" She raised her right arm above her head. "Abba!"

He looked up, hesitated, and then was running too, his arms outstretched in her direction. They collided in a hug, his muscled arms pulling her tight against his broad chest. She buried her face in his cloak and breathed in. His chin rested upon the top of her head.

"Abba," she whispered. "Abba."

After a long while, his hands gripped her upper arms and he held her away from him, his eyes searching her face. Tears tracked his cheeks. "You are well." It wasn't a question.

"I am well."

"You are happy."

"I am happy, Abba."

His gaze lifted, and she knew without looking that Ethan and Levi had caught up to them.

"Menes," Abba said, then corrected himself. "Ethan, my son. You kept them safe. As you promised."

Dobah's pulse skipped at her abba's term of affection. Her letter home—telling of Ethan's welcome into the Jewish community as a convert and their desire to marry—had reached him, and he had replied with a blessing. Still, it made her heart happy to see the warmth in his eyes and hear it in his voice.

"As I promised," Ethan answered.

"We did not know you were coming." Abba's gaze returned to Dobah. "What has changed?"

"Adonai called Yosef and Miryam out of Egypt. We came with them."

Again Abba looked away from her. This time, she knew, he sought her cousin and his family.

"They are no longer with us, Abba. Yosef did not feel safe in the shadow of Jerusalem."

"Within sight of Archelaus," Abba said with a grim nod.

"Yes."

"And so they have gone home to Galilee. To Nazareth."

"Yes."

"That is wise." He looked toward the rooftops of Bethlehem before putting an arm around her shoulders. "Come. Your imma will not forgive me if I do not hasten to take you home. She will want to hear everything about the wedding. And we must reintroduce ourselves to our grandson."

A short while later, they passed a house on the fringe of the village. It was the home of Bilha and Gershom, a couple Dobah had known most of her life. Bilha was in the yard, grinding grain.

"Look who has come back to us," Abba called.

Dobah lifted a hand to wave but was stopped by the look on Bilha's face. A look of utter emptiness, complete devastation. "Abba?"

He didn't slow his steps but kept her moving resolutely forward.

And then she remembered Bilha's son, a boy of not yet two the last time Dobah had seen him, and she heard Yosef's voice relaying the news in Alexandria. *"Of all the sons of Bethlehem under the age of two...only Levi survived."*

She felt it then, the pall that lay over her village all these months later. Tears began to fall, and she lowered her eyes to the ground, not wanting to meet the gazes of any more parents, not wanting to see their losses, a loss that might have been hers if not for the quick actions of her abba and Ethan. She had cried when the news about all that had happened arrived in Egypt, but she hadn't felt the full weight of it until now. How could Bethlehem ever be the same?

Her spirits were lifted somewhat when she saw her imma and was wrapped in another warm embrace. And then she was hugged by Savta. Her elderly grandmother had grown even more frail during Dobah's absence, but her toothless smile was as bright as ever.

Pressing her gnarly fingers against Dobah's cheek, Savta said, "Praise be to Adonai. I feared I would not live long enough to see you again. Now…" She turned toward Ethan. "Now I will know your husband."

"You know him, Savta. He was with the magi, and he worked with Abba before we…before Levi and I went to Egypt."

"I know all that. I have not lost my memories." Her savta waved a hand in dismissal. "But he is not the man he was a year ago. Am I not right?"

Ethan stepped forward. "You are right, good lady."

"I am your savta too."

"Savta," he repeated softly.

While Ethan was usually able to school his expressions to hide his emotions, he didn't attempt to do so now. Dobah saw how moved he was by the acceptance of her family, and her heart welled with love for everyone in the room.

Holding a sleeping Levi in his arms, Ethan paused at the top of the steps outside the kataluma, the guest room that would be home to his little family for the foreseeable future. His throat remained tight with emotion. Boaz and Machla had welcomed him like a son. It didn't surprise him so much as overwhelm him. He hadn't known a father or mother since he was a young child, and he'd never known the tenderness of a grandmother. While he and Yosef had become friends in Egypt, and now Ethan had Dobah for a wife and Levi for a son, this response from his in-laws made him marvel anew at the goodness of God.

He carried Levi into the kataluma and laid him on the cot, pausing long enough to sweep hair off the little boy's forehead. Love welled within his chest. *Bless and protect him, Adonai. Make Your light shine upon him and be gracious to him.*

After straightening, he moved to the narrow window and stared up at the eastern sky. Stars twinkled against the black canopy of night, and they caused him to recall the single bright star that brought him to Bethlehem...and to a newborn King...and to a faith...and to a family...and to a home.

"Ethan?"

He turned and watched Dobah enter the room, an oil lamp in her hand, the flickering light painting her face in shades of gold. "I was remembering the star that brought me here." He glanced toward the window again. "Strange. It seems long ago. Longer than it was. So much has happened since then."

She came to stand beside him, and they turned in unison to look through the window at the stars. He put an arm around her, drawing her close to his side.

"Do you think they'll be all right tonight?" Dobah asked softly.

He didn't have to ask whom she meant. "Yosef will keep them safe."

"I wonder what the future holds for them. I wish I knew more of what the Scriptures tell us about the promised Messiah. Even the rabbis do not always agree, it seems."

"Perhaps you and I could study together."

Dobah pressed her head against his shoulder. "I would like that, Ethan."

It struck him then, a feeling of surprise and wonder. How many khabirs were there who cared if an apprentice could read and write?

Khufu, his master, had insisted Ethan learn to do both and not in one language only. Ethan's unexpected education, while not formal, had enabled him to become a khabir himself while still a young man, and being a khabir had brought him eventually to Bethlehem. The ability to read had allowed him to study in the synagogue in Alexandria, which then allowed him to become one of Adonai's people, which in turn allowed him to become Dobah's husband and a part of her family.

Adonai's hand had surely been upon him from long ago.

CHAPTER TWENTY-FIVE

Dobah stood in the doorway of her parents' house, holding the water jar against her abdomen. She had volunteered to go to the well this morning, but suddenly she wished she hadn't. How many women would she meet who had lost a son on that wretched night nearly a year before? How many women whose wounds remained raw and exposed?

Her imma's hand alighted on Dobah's shoulder. "They will be glad to see you."

"Will they?" She met Imma's gaze. "Would I if I were in their place?"

"Yes, you would be glad too. Perhaps through tears, but you would be glad for them."

"If not for Ethan's quick actions..." She let the words drift into silence.

"I know. I think of it often and thank Adonai for His mercy."

Dobah drew a slow breath and released it. "Imma, there is something we did not tell you in all the excitement of our return."

"You are with child."

Her eyes widened. "How did you know?"

Imma smiled. "Something in your expression as we ate supper last night. I saw it and I knew."

"It is early yet."

"I will pray for you. That you will be well, and our new grandchild will be safely delivered when the time comes."

Dobah pressed her head against her imma's shoulder. "I am glad Adonai sent us home again. We found a good community in Alexandria and were content, but I longed for you and Abba all the same."

"I rejoice over your return, my daughter." She kissed the top of Dobah's head. "Now go. Fetch the water. See your friends and let them welcome you back."

Dobah offered her imma a fleeting smile before leaving the house in the weak light of dawn. The walk to the well was not a long one, and soon she was joined by other women.

"Dobah, we heard you had returned."

"Welcome back, Dobah."

"Congratulations on your marriage. We are eager to meet your husband."

For all the smiles and words of welcome, Dobah remained aware of the blanket of sadness covering the mothers and grandmothers of Bethlehem. How could it be otherwise? It was not quite a year since many of them had seen sons and grandsons die at the hands of Herod's soldiers.

Bilha, whom Dobah had seen the previous day, was already at the well when she and the other women arrived, and when Bilha saw Dobah, her eyes filled with tears. Leaving her full water jar on the edge of the well, she approached Dobah. For a moment, everyone seemed to hold their breaths. Then Bilha reached out and drew Dobah into an embrace.

"It is good you are back," she whispered.

Dobah's throat was almost too thick to answer, "Thank you."

Bilha drew back. "Levi, he is well?"

"Yes."

"And Yosef and Miryam and Yeshua?"

"They are well too. They have returned to Nazareth."

Bilha's gaze lifted in the direction of her home. "Lucky Miryam."

"And you, Bilha? How are you?"

Bilha hesitated a moment then answered, "'Out of the depths I cry to You, O Lord. Lord, hear my voice. Let Your ears be attentive to my cry for mercy.'" She stopped and drew a breath before adding, "'I wait for the Lord, my whole being waits, and in His word I put my hope.'"

Tears streaked Dobah's cheeks.

The other women around the well added their voices to Bilha's. "'Israel, put your hope in the Lord, for with the Lord is unfailing love and with Him is full redemption. He Himself will redeem Israel from all their sins.'"

While the blanket of sadness remained upon the small gathering, Dobah sensed hope had entered in. How they could mingle in one place—sadness and hope—she didn't know, but it happened all the same.

"Will you bring Levi to see me?" Bilha asked.

"If you wish it, of course."

"I wish it." Bilha turned away, lifted her water jar to her shoulder, and with soft words of farewell, walked away from the well.

Ellush, a friend of Dobah's imma, stepped close to Dobah's side. "They have prayed for another baby, but Adonai has yet to answer."

Dobah resisted the impulse to cover her belly with her hand. "I will pray too."

"Come. Get your water, and we will walk to your home together. You must tell me all about Alexandria. Is it as large as I have heard? What of its lighthouse? Was it visible from where you lived?"

Dobah smiled as she filled her jar with water from the well and knew she would be required to say very little when she was with Ellush.

It surprised Dobah in the days and weeks that followed, how quickly life fell into old, familiar rhythms. She worked beside her imma, preparing the meals, cleaning the house, grinding grain, baking bread, tending the small garden, milking the goats, mending and washing clothes. She bathed and dressed and fed Levi, and she told him stories of Adonai's people, the stories she had learned as a child. Stories of Avraham and Yitz'chak and Ya'akov. Stories of Yosef in Egypt. Stories of Moshe and the exodus. Stories of Yonah and the whale.

Ethan went to work in the vineyard with her abba, seemingly as content to learn this new trade as he had been to learn stonework and carpentry from Yosef. How many men were willing to change their lives so drastically, not once but twice in a single year?

Ethan's thirst for knowledge and understanding of the Living God remained as great as it had been in Alexandria, and he made good on his invitation for Dobah to study with him. Several times each week, Ethan went to the synagogue and read from the scrolls.

Then he returned home and shared all he had learned. Within the sacred writings, they found answers but also came away with more questions.

The prophet Mikhah told them that from Bethlehem would come One who would be an anointed ruler in Israel, sent by Adonai. Although His parents were from Nazareth, Yeshua had been born in Bethlehem because of the Roman census.

The prophet Yirmeyahu told them of a massacre, Rachel weeping for her children, refusing to be comforted because they were no more. Dobah and Ethan had experienced that night for themselves.

The prophet Hoshea told them the Messiah would spend a portion of His youth in Egypt. This, too, they had seen with their own eyes. "And out of Egypt I called my son," the prophet had written. Yeshua had been sent to Egypt, and Yeshua had been called out of Egypt.

"No wonder King Herod was afraid of a little baby," Ethan said one evening as they walked home. "It was all foretold. Yeshua is the Anointed One, the coming King."

"King," Dobah whispered. "I do not understand how that can be. He is the son of a tekton. He is the child of an ordinary family."

"He is so much more than that, Dobah."

She knew her husband was right. Yet it was difficult to believe that the baby who had been born in a stable—the infant she'd watched nursing in his imma's arms in Alexandria, that little boy who had learned to walk and talk like any other child of his age—was destined to be a king.

As if reading her mind, Ethan said, "King David began life as a shepherd boy, the youngest of eight sons. But he became Adonai's anointed king. Is anything impossible for El Shaddai?"

She stopped walking, forcing Ethan to do the same. "No, nothing is impossible for Him. And yet I do not understand how it can be so, knowing my cousin, knowing his wife."

"I heard Miryam say once that she pondered many things in her heart. Perhaps we must do the same as we wait."

"Perhaps," she responded. Silently, she added, *Adonai, help me to see what You are doing.*

CHAPTER TWENTY-SIX

In the month of Nisan, 3 BC

Although Yosef had said he would come to Jerusalem for Pesach, Dobah wasn't certain he would actually do so. Less than two months had passed since the two families parted ways near Ashkelon. Would Yosef undertake the journey from Nazareth to Jerusalem so soon after arriving home again? Besides, Archelaus still ruled Judea. Was the danger any less now than it had been before? Perhaps he would come without Miryam and Yeshua. Many men from other regions left their wives and children behind when attending the festivals. Yosef might do so this year. Still, Dobah hoped she would see him and his family this Pesach.

Two days before the beginning of the festival, Dobah and Levi returned from the vineyard after taking lunch to Ethan and Abba. From the vantage point of a hillside, she could see one of the main roads leading to Jerusalem. It was filled with pilgrims on their way to the holy city as well as to other nearby villages. Tents were popping up outside the walls of the city to house those who were without friends or family to take them in. Bethlehem was also bursting at the seams, just as it had at the time of the census. But this annual festival was a more joyous and sacred reason for everyone to gather.

In midstep, Levi plopped down on the ground, apparently fascinated by some poppies growing on the hillside. With a soft laugh, Dobah joined him. She plucked one of the wildflowers and tried to slide it behind her son's ear, but he would have none of it, jerking away and protesting with a loud, "No! No!" So instead she wove the flower into her own hair before leaning back on her hands and turning her face toward the sun. She smiled, enjoying the peace of the spring afternoon. Even more, enjoying this moment of rest.

Tomorrow, on the fourteenth day of Nisan, Abba would take his family to the temple to sacrifice the lamb that would then be roasted for their Seder meal. Today and tomorrow would be busy ones for Dobah and her imma. She sighed, knowing she should get home. Yet she remained, luxuriating in the sweet spring day.

"Imma!" Levi's hands slapped her rounded abdomen. "Imma!"

Her eyes opened. "What?" She grabbed his pudgy hands with her own and pulled them to her lips.

"Imma!" Levi looked over his shoulder.

Dobah followed his gaze, and there they were—Yosef, Miryam, and Yeshua—standing on the pathway below her.

"Yosef!" She scrambled to her feet, bringing Levi into her arms once she stood. "Miryam! You came."

"I told you we would," her cousin answered.

"I know. But it's so far, and you only just returned to Nazareth. I was afraid you would change your mind."

"Will there be space at your abba's table for us during Pesach?"

"You know there will be." She hurried down the gentle incline. "There is always room at our table for you. And room in our home for you to stay as well."

"Your abba is a generous man."

"Would you like to see him before I take you to the house?" She glanced in the direction of the vineyard. "He and Ethan are working."

Yosef's arm went around Miryam's shoulders. "I think we must wait to see them. We have walked far today."

"Then come. Imma and I will see to your needs."

As they started walking in the direction of Bethlehem, Dobah's mind flooded with questions, but she bit them back. She could see the exhaustion on their faces. There would be plenty of time for talk later. The festival lasted for seven days, after all.

Happiness flooded through her. Seven days with her cousin and his wife. She'd missed seeing them on a daily basis, as had been true in Egypt, but she hadn't known how much until she'd seen them on the path at the bottom of that hillside.

When they entered the village a short while later, Yosef's expression became grim, and Dobah understood. He and Miryam had left Bethlehem several days before Herod's soldiers came, but he knew what had happened in this place. He remembered the people who lived here, and he remembered the children who were no more.

There is so much evil in the world, Adonai. Why didn't You protect all the sons of Bethlehem that night?

Startled by her thoughts, she pressed a hand to her breastbone. It seemed wrong to question the Living God in such a way. But was it wrong? King David had poured out his feelings in his songs. Questions. Anger. Sorrow. Dread. Devotion. Praise. It was all there. Did Adonai welcome her to be as honest with Him as David had been?

"Machla!" Yosef shouted, bringing Dobah out of her deep thoughts.

Her cousin hurried forward and embraced Imma where she stood near the garden. Soon Miryam did the same. Dobah stood back, watching the happy reunion and knowing it would be repeated as soon as Abba and Ethan returned from the vineyard.

"Come," Imma said. "We will get you settled."

"Are we the first to arrive?" Yosef asked.

"We are not sure who to expect for Pesach this year. Aharon and Baruch are staying in Bethany with Uncle Caleb." As Imma led Yosef and Miryam into the house, her voice faded away.

"Go!" Levi demanded. "Go!"

Dobah laughed before hurrying after the others.

On the following afternoon, Ethan carried Levi as the family walked toward Jerusalem. Ahead of Ethan, Boaz carried the unblemished lamb that would be sacrificed for his household. Dobah walked by Ethan's side, and behind them came the rest of the family—Machla, Yosef, Miryam, and Yeshua. Only Savta had remained at home, her age making it difficult to join them.

In the distance, the temple complex dominated the city skyline, a gleaming beacon of white and gold. Ethan's pulse quickened at the sight. This was his first Pesach as a ger tzedek, and the importance of the upcoming rituals filled him with wonder, particularly the sacrifice of the paschal lamb and the meal that would take place this evening at the start of Pesach.

The road leading to the southern gate was packed with pilgrims. Many men came alone, others came with their families. Voices were raised in conversation, and the bleating of lambs added to the cacophony that filled the air.

Ethan had peppered both his father-in-law and Yosef with many questions about Pesach. Although his role today was simply to observe, still he wanted to understand all that would transpire. Especially with the masses surrounding them. Though this wasn't the first time he'd visited the temple since Dobah and he returned from Egypt, it was still difficult for him to imagine how the temple complex could hold all the people pushing forward through the gates of the city.

"What are you thinking?" Dobah asked, looking up at him. When he told her, she smiled. "You will see."

Ethan didn't have long to wait. When they reached the Temple Mount, he soon witnessed the skilled organizational process that managed the mass of people efficiently.

Boaz, as head of his household, took the lamb forward into the crowded temple courtyard. It was there he sacrificed the lamb. Priests were nearby to collect the lamb's blood in a sacred vessel. Afterward, they passed the vessels along a line of other priests until the last priest sprinkled the blood on the base of the altar. Only then was the lamb given back to Boaz, who quickly returned to his family. Then they began the walk home, where a special oven awaited the lamb for roasting.

As they headed toward Bethlehem, part of a sea of people moving both toward and away from Jerusalem, Ethan thought of that dead lamb in Boaz's arms. Because of the blood of the lamb, the angel of death had passed over the Israelites in Egypt.

The blood of the lamb. The words seemed to reverberate in his chest. Why, he didn't know.

After sunset that night, Ethan gathered with the rest of the family around a low table. In the center was lamb, cooked just as prescribed by the Torah. Along with the lamb and unleavened bread were bitter herbs, to symbolize the bitterness of slavery; the *charoset*, a sweet paste, to symbolize the mortar the Israelites used as slaves; the parsley dipped in salt water to represent their tears; a shank bone to symbolize the sacrifice; and a roasted egg to represent mourning and the cycle of life.

During the meal, the story of the Exodus was retold. Cups of wine were drunk to symbolize redemption and freedom. Prayers were prayed and songs were sung. Everything about the meal had meaning. And every meaning seemed to touch his heart and make him thankful to be a part of it.

Ethan would remember this day and this night, his first Pesach as a righteous convert, for as long as he lived. Should Adonai will it, he would celebrate this festival again and again throughout his lifetime. In another two or three years, Levi would be old enough to ask why this night was different from all other nights. A few years beyond that and the child Dobah carried now would have that honor. Perhaps Ethan would even live long enough to hear his grandchildren ask the question.

At that thought, he smiled. It would be better if he concentrated on the here and now—and let the tomorrows tend to themselves.

CHAPTER TWENTY-SEVEN

Six months later, in the month of Tishri, 3 BC

"Dobah." Imma's voice stopped her near the doorway. "I will get the water this morning. You should rest."

Dobah turned, feeling awkward and as large as a whale. "I feel better when I am active."

"You could have the baby at any time."

"I know, Imma. I had a baby before. Remember?" She smiled to hide her impatience. She was tired of everyone asking her how she felt and watching her expectantly. "It is only a walk to the well, and the water jar is no heavier than Levi. I still carry him when I need to."

Imma pressed her lips together, obviously restraining herself from saying more.

Dobah gave a nod, clutched the water jug against her side, and left the house. The gray light of dawn still lay over the village, and when she met other women also walking toward the well, they spoke to one another in hushed tones, not wanting to break the quiet of early morning.

Bilha was first at the well, as was often the case, and she greeted Dobah with a smile, her hands resting on the swell of her own belly. Joy seemed to radiate from her, and Dobah thanked Adonai for the longed-for child Bilha carried. The pregnancy had brought her friend out of a dark place, and she rejoiced with her.

Bilha held out a hand. "Let me fill that for you."

Dobah didn't try to argue with Bilha, the way she had with Imma. In truth, bending over to fill the water jug was almost more than she could handle.

"Gershom says the grape harvest will be finished today."

"That is what Abba said last night." She put a hand to the small of her back and drew a slow breath. "It has been an abundant harvest. My abba is pleased. Adonai be praised."

"Are you all right, Dobah?"

She started to answer, but the breath caught in her throat as pain tightened her lower abdomen and curved around to her spine. A soft gasp escaped her.

"You are *not* all right." Bilha set down the water jug. "We must get you home."

The pain began to ease. "I should still take the water. Imma will—"

"Do not worry." Bilha glanced at the other women around them. "We will make certain there is plenty of water available for your imma." She put an arm around Dobah's back. "Now, let us go. We will walk slowly."

Dobah nodded. The pain was gone, but she suspected it would return before long.

Softly, Bilha began to sing a song of David. "'For You created my inmost being; You knit me together in my mother's womb. I praise You because I am fearfully and wonderfully made; Your works are wonderful, I know that full well.'"

Dobah felt another twinge in her abdomen but managed to join her voice to Bilha's. "'My frame was not hidden from You when I was made in the secret place, when I was woven together in the depths of the earth. Your eyes saw my unformed body; all the days ordained for me were written in Your book before one of them came to be.'" She gasped as the twinge became something stronger.

The song forgotten, Bilha's grip tightened, and she hurried their steps.

Oppressive afternoon heat pressed upon Dobah as she lay on the bed in the kataluma, her labor intense. Her imma and sisters were in attendance, and the worried expressions they exchanged did nothing to reassure Dobah that the end was anywhere in sight.

Hadassah placed a damp cloth on Dobah's forehead, but there was no coolness in it. Irritably, Dobah pushed the cloth away as another pain began. She moaned as the discomfort built to its crescendo. Unable to hold it back, a cry tore from her lips. When the pain subsided, Dobah caught her breath even as she fought back tears.

"Imma, it is not like before," she whispered.

"Every birth is different, my daughter."

"Levi rushed to be born. Remember?"

"I remember. I almost did not catch him in time."

"This baby is in no hurry." Dobah closed her eyes. "And I am tired."

Imma leaned close. "Your time to rest will come, but it is not here yet."

Dobah nodded.

Dobah's sister Leah took up the water jar and started for the door. "I will get fresh water."

Dobah could have told her not to bother. The room was too warm for it to stay cool for long.

"And," Leah added, "I will let Ethan know he has a long wait ahead."

"Ethan is here?" Dobah looked at her imma.

"He is here. Your abba sent him home as soon as they received word."

"The harvest…"

"Ethan is only one of many working to bring in the last of the grapes. Do not worry. The harvest will be completed, and your abba will rush home to see his newest grandchild."

Another pain took hold, and Dobah couldn't form a response.

While Boaz sat on a stool, his back resting against the wall, Ethan paced the length of the living area. Every sound from the kataluma drew his gaze up the stairs to the door of that room.

"You should eat something," his father-in-law said.

"I could not eat."

"We could be waiting all night."

Ethan turned toward Boaz. "All night? But it has been hours already." It seemed more than hours. It seemed like days, even weeks.

Women died in childbirth. He knew that. Babies died in childbirth. He knew that too. But until this moment, he'd never considered anything could go wrong with his wife or with his child. Dobah was young and strong. She had already given birth to Levi, who was a lively, intelligent, healthy little boy. Why should Ethan worry?

He worried anyway.

Adonai, You are righteous and just. Turn Your face toward my family and be gracious to them. Make Your face to shine upon them.

He began pacing again. He had reached the steps that led down into the stable area when a loud cry from the upper room yanked him around. After a heartbeat, he ran toward the stairs.

"No, Ethan." Boaz's strong hand gripped Ethan's upper arm. "The women will send for us when it is time."

"But—"

"They will send for us when it is time," Boaz repeated, more gently this time.

Ethan nodded with reluctance. He wanted to see his wife. He needed to know she was okay. But he knew Boaz was right. Looking at his father-in-law, he asked, "You did this three times?"

As Boaz sat once again, he chuckled. "I did, and I survived the wait. Men are useless at such times."

At that moment, Levi ran out of his great-grandmother's room, a favorite toy in his hand, and threw himself into Boaz's lap. Refreshed by his nap, the little boy was oblivious to what was transpiring in the upper room. He cared only about sitting with his saba. Even when he heard his imma's moan, he seemed undisturbed by it.

He trusts, as we all must trust. Ethan walked to where his father-in-law and stepson sat against the wall. Reaching out, he ruffled the little boy's thick, curly hair. "I need to be more like you, my son."

The words had just left his mouth when another sound came from upstairs, this one the shrill cry of a newborn. Ethan turned to look at the closed door. Boaz stood beside him, Levi in his arms. As they stared upward, the door opened, and Leah appeared, looking hot and weary but smiling broadly.

"All is well," she told them. "Ethan, you have a healthy daughter."

"Adonai be praised," Boaz said.

A daughter. A healthy daughter. And Dobah was well. "Adonai be praised."

CHAPTER TWENTY-EIGHT

Two weeks later, Dobah awakened early as daylight seeped into the upper room through the narrow window. When she rolled her head to the side, she saw Ethan standing over his daughter where she slept in a basket. His position was such and the light was enough that she could see the rapt expression on his face. He was besotted with Rachel, the name they had chosen for her.

Dobah was thankful the naming of a daughter didn't include a fixed day or a specific ritual, as was the case for sons. Levi's circumcision and naming ceremony had been a sad time for her. Joyous too, but she'd been so aware of the absence of her husband. So afraid she would always be without a husband at her side.

And now there was Ethan. She never could have dreamed of meeting such a man, of marrying such a man, of loving such a man and being loved by him in return.

"Good morning, Husband," she whispered.

He turned and approached the bedside. "I thought you might sleep awhile longer."

Dobah yawned. "I had forgotten what the first weeks with an infant are like."

"Then go back to sleep." He leaned down and kissed her forehead. "I will see you when I return from the vineyard." Quietly, he slipped from the room.

Dobah closed her eyes, hoping sleep would return. When it did not, she rose and prepared for the day. By the time she was washed and dressed, the baby was stirring, ready to be nursed again. Soon, Levi would be awake as well. And judging by the sounds from downstairs, her imma was busy with her morning chores after feeding the men and seeing them off to work.

When at last she descended the stairs, carrying Rachel in one arm and holding Levi's hand with the other, full sunlight spilled through the open doorway, and the interior of the house held the promise of another hot day. Imma kneaded bread and hummed to herself, and Savta sat near the doorway, mending a tunic.

"Good morning, Imma. Savta."

"Good morning," the two older women answered in unison.

"How can I help?" Even as she asked the question, she knew what her imma's answer would be.

"Sit and tend the children. I have everything in hand."

A rap on the doorjamb drew their gazes to the front entrance as Hadassah entered the house. "Have you heard?" Dobah's sister asked.

"Heard what?"

"More Roman soldiers arrived in Jerusalem yesterday. The women were talking about it at the well this morning."

Imma smacked the lump of dough with a fist, as if that were her reply to Hadassah's news.

Star of Wonder: Dobah's Story

"The Romans are always sending new soldiers to the garrison." Dobah ran her fingers over the dark hair on her daughter's head. "That is nothing worth talking about."

"There are whispers about the Messiah arriving during the Feast of Booths. Perhaps the Romans are preparing for trouble because of it."

Dobah met her imma's gaze across the room.

Imma said, "There are always whispers about the Messiah. That is not new either."

Yeshua was less than two years old and living in Nazareth. Even if he was brought to Jerusalem by his parents for Sukkot, what need was there for more Romans in Jerusalem? But thoughts of Herod's soldiers on that dreadful night in Bethlehem caused her to shiver. Yeshua—and others—weren't safe just because they were young. Those in power could do dreadful things.

Worry began to gnaw at Dobah's insides. Because of Rachel's birth, Dobah was prohibited from participating in the religious activities of the festival. While the rest of her family and community would go to Jerusalem, she would observe the Feast of Booths in a limited way at home. Abba and Ethan would build a sukkah nearby so she could participate as much as the ritual purity laws allowed. But she wouldn't be part of the pilgrimage to the temple.

Again, she shivered, more unsettled by the news of the soldiers than she wanted to admit.

Ethan and Gad, one of Boaz's workmen, walked toward Jerusalem, Gad leading a donkey pulling the cart. Once again the roads were filled with pilgrims, this time coming to the city for the weeklong observance of Sukkot, a festival that would begin in a couple of days. While Ethan looked forward to the celebration of another feast and his ability to observe it in the temple in Jerusalem, his excitement was dimmed somewhat by the restrictions placed on Dobah. She would have to remain at home with their daughter. She said she didn't mind, but he would miss her by his side all the same.

As they walked through the gate into the city, the sound of many voices seemed to double. People all around him talking, added to animal sounds—the bleat of sheep, the cooing of doves—made his head begin to pound.

"Which way to the pottery shop?" he asked Gad, raising his voice to be heard above all the other sounds.

Gad pointed to a street to the left, and they proceeded in that direction. Ethan was thankful the shop was away from the temple. The street was less crowded than before.

Their errand this morning was to pick up an order for thirty more *amphorae*—large clay jars used to store wine. For more than fifteen years, Boaz had purchased the amphorae his vineyard required from Lemuel, a Jew originally from Tyre, and had nothing but good things to say about the potter and the quality of his work.

The narrow street wound its way through parts of the city Ethan had yet to visit in the months since his return from Egypt. He was thankful for Gad's presence. Otherwise, he might have become lost.

Lemuel's pottery shop was larger than Ethan expected. That the man owned a successful business was obvious, given its size and the amount of merchandise on display.

"So you are Boaz's son-in-law." Lemuel grasped Ethan's wrist and grinned. "I am honored to know you."

"And you," Ethan responded.

"I have the order all ready. My sons will help load it into your cart."

Ethan thanked him.

"It was a good harvest, I hear." As Lemuel spoke, he motioned with his hand, and two younger men—who bore a striking resemblance to him as well as to each other—began to carry jars out of the shop's interior. Gad did the same.

"This was my first year to be present for the harvest," Ethan answered, "but yes, Boaz says it has been very good. Now he prays for rain in the weeks to come."

Lemuel nodded. "We all pray for the rain in this season. May Adonai bless us with an abundance of it. After the booths come down, of course."

"Of course." Ethan chuckled then took out the coin purse and paid the potter for the jars.

Once the amphorae were loaded and secured in the cart, Ethan bid Lemuel and his sons a good day, and he and Gad began the walk back to Bethlehem. Since Gad was a mostly silent companion, Ethan let his mind wander to his newborn daughter.

It still amazed him, the feelings that welled inside when he looked at Rachel. A love so strong it seemed almost violent. He would do anything to protect her, to keep her safe, to help her grow up strong. He understood in an entirely new way how Dobah must have felt on the night they'd fled Bethlehem before Herod's soldiers could find them.

"Thank You," he whispered beneath his breath.

Just ahead of them, the street they followed joined with two other streets, and soon they were plunged into the crowd of people—residents and pilgrims—moving this way and that.

"Out of the way!"

The shout came from behind Ethan. He turned and discovered three Roman soldiers on horseback pushing straight toward him, the people parting before them as quickly as possible. One of the Romans brandished a whip, and he used it upon the crowd rather than upon his horse.

"Out of the way!"

Ethan's donkey chose that moment to become stubborn. He planted his hooves and refused to move. Ethan joined Gad at the head of the donkey, pulling on his bridle to no avail. Ethan raised a hand as he looked at the soldiers, wanting to wave off the approaching horses, silently pleading for them to go around the donkey and cart that had stopped directly in their path.

"Move, you dog!"

The whip came down toward Ethan's head. Instinctively, he grabbed it and then swept it away from him. Chaos erupted all around. Screams split the air. Something hard hit Ethan on the back of the head. He tried to turn, to strike back, but a second hit knocked him to the ground. Then all went black.

CHAPTER TWENTY-NINE

It was early in the afternoon when Dobah's abba stepped through the door. An odd time of day for him to make an appearance at home. Odder still that he was alone. But it was the grave look in his eyes and the hard line of his mouth that caused alarm to shoot through her.

She rose from the stool, the mending falling to the floor near the basket where Rachel was sleeping. "Abba?"

"Daughter." He crossed the room and placed a hand on her shoulder. Something in his manner reminded her of the day he'd brought the news about Dover.

Her pulse pounded in her ears. "Is it Ethan?"

He nodded.

"What has happened?" This question came out a mere whisper. "Was there...was there an accident?"

"Ethan has been arrested by the Romans."

"Arrested?" She shook her head, trying to rid the confusion. "But why? What did he do?"

"He and Gad went to Jerusalem to get the last order of amphorae. Ethan got in the way of some Roman soldiers. I am unsure of the charge. Gad was not able to tell me much."

"They let Gad go?"

Her abba nodded again.

"What will we do?"

"*We* will do nothing. *I* will go to Jerusalem and see what can be done."

"Abba." The word was a cry for help.

He gathered her into a close embrace, his chin resting on the crown of her head, her head against his chest. "It will be all right, Dobah. You will see. It will be all right."

Listening to his heartbeat, she remembered again when he'd told her of Dover's accident. But Ethan wasn't dead. He was in the hands of the Romans. The hated Romans. Romans who despised the people of Israel. What might they do to him in a prison cell?

She pulled her head back to look up. "Please let me go with you."

"I cannot let you come, Dobah. You have your children to think of. You must care for them. I cannot risk—" He broke off abruptly.

Fear shivered through her, understanding suddenly that Abba would put himself in danger by asking about Ethan. Imma came to join them, her face creased with a worry that matched Dobah's. She put an arm around both of them and bowed her head. Although Imma made no sound, Dobah knew she was praying. After a long while, Boaz drew back. His gaze met his wife's then his daughter's. Finally, without a word, he turned and left the house.

"Imma…" Dobah drew a shallow breath. "What if neither of them comes home again?"

Her imma touched Dobah's cheek with cool fingertips. "Adonai gives and Adonai takes away. Blessed be the name of Adonai."

Dobah took no comfort from the words, despite knowing they were true and that she should rest in them.

Rachel stirred, alerting Dobah it would be time to nurse her soon. She went to the basket and looked down at her baby. Rachel was only two weeks old. Would she never know Ethan, just as Levi would never know Dover?

Adonai, protect them. Send Ethan and Abba home to us.

She lifted her daughter from the basket and began to sway back and forth, her eyes closed. Words from a psalm rose to her lips, and she spoke them aloud. "'Give thanks to the Lord, for He is good. His love endures forever.'" Her imma's voice joined hers. "'Give thanks to the God of gods. His love endures forever.'" Spoken words changed to singing until they had praised Adonai through every verse.

And then, as so often was true for women, all they could do was wait.

Ethan sat on the stone floor of the cell. Somewhere beyond the iron bars, a torch burned in a narrow passage, and it shed a little light into the space Ethan occupied. The air was damp, and the horrible smells of the prison made him sick to his stomach. Or perhaps he was sick from the blows he'd taken to his head and torso. Had that been hours ago or days ago? He wasn't sure.

Scratching sounds on the opposite side of the cell drew his gaze. Not that he could see anything in the darkness, but he knew it must be rats. How long before one of them ran across his legs or tried to take a bite out of his arm? He shuddered. He would rather face a lion or a bear than a rat.

Pain flared again in his head, and he reached back to gently touch the spot where he'd first been hit. Not by a human fist. He was convinced of that. Something harder had been used to knock him to the ground. A knot had formed on the back of his skull, and the congealed blood felt sticky against his fingertips.

Thirst made him lick his lips, but he didn't want to call out for water. If there was a bucket of it somewhere in the bowels of this prison, it would be as filthy as everything else. Rats would have been there too. His stomach roiled at the thought.

A cry sounded from somewhere far away. Or at least he thought it was far away. A man in pain. Or perhaps a man gone insane.

Ethan feared insanity might close in on him too. He'd spent the bulk of his life traveling across vast stretches of land, sleeping under an open sky. This dark confinement was torture, far worse than the blow to his head or the booted kicks he'd received. And what had he done to deserve any of it? He'd replayed the scene in his mind many times since regaining consciousness, and he did not understand. All he'd wanted was to avoid a collision between horse and cart. Anyone with eyes could have seen the donkey was the problem. A stubborn donkey, the crowded street, and Romans riding their horses too fast.

He heard a voice then, someone who seemed to be approaching his cell while speaking to himself or someone else. Ethan got to his feet and, with a hand pressed against his aching side, moved closer to the barred door, hungry for the sight of another living soul. To his surprise and relief, the man walked straight to his cell, holding a torch high over his head. Ethan shielded his eyes against the light.

"Stand away from the door," his jailer said, his voice gruff.

Ethan stepped back, his heart beginning to pound along with his head, and watched as the man placed a key in the lock and turned it. As the door creaked open, he had to fight the urge to lunge forward.

"All right. Let's go." The jailer motioned with his free hand for Ethan to go before him through the narrow passage.

The climb out of the prison seemed to take forever, but eventually the blackness and the smells gave way to daylight and fresh air. Ethan stopped before stepping through the final doorway and breathed in deeply.

A hand from behind gave him a shove. "Get on with you."

Ethan looked over his shoulder, suddenly uncertain. Was he headed for freedom or something worse than the time he'd spent in captivity?

Another shove caused him to stumble out into the courtyard. Somehow, he kept from falling to his knees, and as he straightened, on the far side of the square, he caught sight of a familiar figure. Boaz!

"Get on with you," the jailer snapped. "You are free to go."

Free. Just like that, he was free? He couldn't believe it. Was afraid to believe it.

Before he could receive another shove, he limped toward his father-in-law, half expecting a hand from behind to grab him and take him back into the prison.

But it was Boaz's hand that grasped Ethan's upper arm and steadied him. "Say nothing," Boaz said in a low voice. "Come with me."

Instinct forced Ethan to keep his head down, his gaze locked on the ground before him, allowing Boaz to steer him through the unfamiliar area and, at last, out into the city. The streets of Jerusalem were not as busy as they had been when last Ethan walked them. The sun was low in the western sky. Sunset was not far away.

"Can you walk back to Bethlehem?" Boaz asked.

"I think so." He lowered the arm that had been pressed against his abdomen, his hand holding his side.

"I am sorry it took so long to get you released."

Again he wondered if he'd been in that cell for hours or days. "What day is it?" he asked softly.

Boaz stopped walking and studied Ethan's face a moment before answering, "The arrest happened this morning."

Hours then. Perhaps ten hours or a little more. Not so very long, but it had seemed an eternity in the disorienting darkness. Ethan released a soft groan as they began to walk again. "I was afraid I never would be free again. I do not even know why I was arrested."

"You endangered the life of a Roman citizen."

"I what?" In his surprise, he shouted the words, and pain shot through his head in response. He shrank back, as if he could escape it.

"That was the charge against you. They say you tried to spook the soldier's horse, endangering the Roman's life. A charge that could have brought execution."

"But it was not like that. I tried to prevent a collision. The donkey would not—"

"Son, it does not matter what really happened. It only matters they let you go."

Ethan halted once again, causing Boaz to do the same. "Why did they let me go?"

Although his father-in-law said nothing, the answer was in his eyes.

"You paid someone for my release."

"Come on," Boaz responded. "It will be dark before we get home, and your wife and imma will be worried about us both."

"Boaz…"

"I did what had to be done, Ethan."

How much? Ethan wondered. How much had Boaz paid to obtain his freedom? His father-in-law was not a poor man, but neither was he rich. However much he'd paid, the money had been taken from another place of need.

"Thank you."

"Adonai will provide," was Boaz's response.

The six miles to Bethlehem felt like a hundred.

CHAPTER THIRTY

Dobah awakened in the night with a start, her heart hammering, fear icing her veins. She reached out in the darkness to touch Ethan. His body was warm. His chest rose and fell in a steady rhythm. Although bruised and sore, he would recover. He would be able to celebrate the Feast of Booths with other members of the family. He would be able to work again. He was safe.

Safe?

Dobah rolled to her other side and touched her sleeping daughter in the basket beside the bed.

Were any of them ever safe? Wherever they went, whatever they did, they remained an occupied nation, ruled by those who despised them. Ethan had done nothing to deserve a beating, let alone to be thrown into prison. And yet that's what had happened.

She should pray. She should worship Adonai. Hadn't He saved Levi from Herod's soldiers? Hadn't He returned Ethan to his family? But her heart felt too cold and weary to pray, too cold and weary to find words of praise. The songs of David told her that Adonai provided all that she needed, that Adonai was with His people even in the valley of the shadow of death. So why didn't it feel that way? Why did she feel alone and afraid? And so angry.

Yes, angry. She wanted her people to be free of those who occupied Israel and oppressed them with taxes and cruelty. She wanted the Messiah to come and set them free. If Yeshua was the Messiah, how long would she have to wait to see Him bring judgment upon the Romans? He wasn't yet two years old. Would she have to wait twenty years? Thirty years? Even longer? Hadn't her people waited long enough?

Ethan could have been killed for doing nothing more than raise his hand as a horse bore down upon a stubborn donkey and a cart filled with clay jars. He could have been kept in prison indefinitely, perhaps forever. He'd been beaten and kicked. He might have been killed outright. They might even have crucified him, a form of execution the Romans had perfected. She could have been widowed a second time. Where was Adonai in the midst of all of it?

Do You not care? Look at us. Do You not care what is happening to Your people?

She rose from the bed and went close to the window that was high up on the wall of the room. Through the narrow opening, she saw stars sprinkling the ebony sky. The teachers of Israel said Adonai had created the heavens and earth, that He'd placed the stars in the sky, that He knew their very numbers. But if so, why didn't He look down upon His people and set them free from the Romans, as He had freed them from the Egyptians? Why did He delay? Why must she wait for Yeshua to grow up before she could see deliverance?

Tears traced her cheeks. She felt their warmth on her skin before she realized she was crying. But it wasn't sorrow she felt. She wanted to raise her fists toward heaven and rage against the injustice surrounding her.

"Dobah?" Ethan's voice was gravelly with sleep.

"I am here."

"Come back to bed."

"I cannot sleep."

"Then come and let me hold you while you tell me what is wrong."

She returned to the bed, but she wouldn't admit to her fears or the anger she felt. They seemed too personal, perhaps even too shameful. Her husband was full of faith. He was not a Jew by birth, as she was, and yet he had more trust in Adonai than she did.

Ethan drew her close, her head resting on his shoulder. "I am all right, Dobah. My bruises will heal."

"I know."

"The time will come," he whispered near her ear.

Perhaps he understood her better than she knew.

His arm tightened around her. "Boaz expects some of your relatives to arrive today. It will be good to see more of your family."

Dobah was certain Yosef would be among her cousins and wondered if he would bring Miryam and Yeshua once again. The law only required the festival pilgrimages of the men of Israel, not the women and children, and the journey from Nazareth was a long one.

Just as the wait for Yeshua to grow up would be a long one.

Protect Him, Adonai. Make Him wise and strong. Give Him the skills He will need to free our people. Your people.

Anxiety coiled in Dobah's belly as she watched her abba and husband leave for the vineyard the next morning. She understood there was much to be done this time of year, that the crushing of the grapes, the making of wine, following the harvest didn't allow them to be idle, especially with Sukkot upon them. Still, it was hard to let either of them out of her sight after what had happened in Jerusalem.

It wasn't until the arrival of Yosef—along with two more of their cousins, Joktan and Chenaniah—that Dobah felt her spirits lift, even if Miryam and little Yeshua were not with them. She hurried outside, Rachel in her arms and Levi holding onto the hem of her tunic.

"Cousins!" she called.

There was the usual exchange of hellos and hugs. The sukkah built beside Boaz's home was admired. Offers of help were extended. And when Imma invited everyone into the house for something to eat and drink, Joktan and Chenaniah were quick to accept the offer. Yosef hung back for a moment and placed his hand on Rachel's head. Softly, he spoke a blessing over her, causing Dobah to blink back tears.

"Is something wrong, Dobah? You do not seem yourself."

She drew a breath then told him, without elaboration, what had transpired the previous day.

"Boaz paid for Ethan's release?" Yosef asked after she fell silent.

"Yes."

"Was it a heavy penalty?"

"I do not know. He did not say. Does it matter?" Dread seeped through her veins.

"There is unrest among our people, and the Romans are uneasy because of it. They are ready to see danger everywhere, even where there is none."

"Are you and Miryam safe where you are? Is Yeshua safe?"

"Strangers seldom come through Nazareth. The village is not on a main road, so the soldiers rarely come there either."

"But Nazareth is in the shadow of Sepphoris and Herod Antipas."

Yosef offered a humorless smile. "No one is looking for the Messiah in Galilee. Not in Nazareth, of all places."

Dobah bent to kiss the top of Rachel's head. "So much has happened in the last two years. I try to be brave, but I am afraid. What if they had not released Ethan? He was in their prison for less than a full day, but they could have kept him. They might have killed him."

"Our people have been subjugated to other nations many times."

"Why does Adonai allow it?" Petulance and anger mingled in her tone.

Yosef lifted Levi into his arms, smiling at the boy. "I do not pretend to know the ways of Adonai, Dobah. I only know He is gracious and loving. He is merciful and just."

Her cousin's answer didn't satisfy Dobah. Her frustration wasn't only because Ethan had been beaten and thrown into prison when he'd done nothing wrong. She was afraid...and she was tired of being afraid. She almost envied the men who became zealots. At least they were doing something. At least they were fighting back against the oppression.

"Dobah?"

She met Yosef's gaze.

"Do not let hatred take over your heart."

She gave him a brief nod, but she wasn't convinced she could change what she felt. Was it wrong to hate the Romans? Didn't all Jews in Israel hate them? Even members of the Sanhedrin who tried hard to keep the peace must hate them in their hearts. Surely they must.

Yosef placed a hand on her shoulder. "The Romans do not care what you feel about them. You do not harm them by hating. You only harm yourself."

She loved Yosef. He was kind and thoughtful. He was her favorite cousin, and she'd always thought him wise, even when he was a boy. But she thought he was wrong about this. Until her fear went away, how could she expect hatred to disappear?

CHAPTER THIRTY-ONE

Several mornings later, halfway through the weeklong Festival of Booths, Dobah sat with her infant daughter in the sukkah. All of the family—her husband and son, her parents, and her cousins—along with their neighbors had gone into Jerusalem, singing words of thanksgiving from the Hallel.

"I will give You thanks, for You answered me."

As she closed her eyes, it was as if she could hear them singing the words and see them walking together, smiling together, rejoicing together. Sukkot was, after all, the most joyous of the Jewish festivals.

"The Lord has done this, and it is marvelous in our eyes."

She could imagine the morning sun reflecting off the gold and white of the temple, so beautiful to behold.

"The Lord has done it this very day; let us rejoice today and be glad."

Dobah sang the words too, but they felt false, perhaps because it was a solitary voice in the temporary structure. But more likely because she found it difficult to rejoice in this day Adonai had made, a day when Romans watched and waited for a reason to bring punishment upon the Jewish people.

"You are my God, and I will praise You; You are my God, and I will exalt You."

She pictured her family moving with the crowd through the streets of Jerusalem to the pool of Siloam and watching as water was drawn from it, water that would then be offered as a libation in a ceremony in the temple. And there would be such a celebration. Sukkot marked the end of the agricultural year in Israel, and it was a time to be joyful altogether, as the Torah commanded.

"Perhaps if I was with them," she said softly, her eyes upon Rachel, who was sleeping peacefully.

Voices from down the street drew her gaze beyond the sukkah. Bethlehem was nearly deserted at this time of day during Sukkot. A few new mothers like her who had yet to go through the purification ceremony had stayed behind. Some of the elderly who found the walk to Jerusalem too strenuous. Perhaps someone who was ill or had been injured.

But then she saw them, through the fabric hanging from the roof of the sukkah to provide a little more privacy and shade. Two Roman soldiers, walking down the street. She dropped onto the mat that served as her bed and pressed herself against a table leg, doing her best to disappear from view. Her heart beat so hard, she feared the soldiers would hear it. But they didn't even look at the sukkah. They appeared completely unconcerned. It made her wonder why they were in Bethlehem if they cared so little about what or who was there.

Moments after the two soldiers had turned a corner, disappearing from view, Rachel began to stir and make small whimpering sounds. With shaking hands, Dobah prepared to nurse her daughter while praying for her family's safe return from Jerusalem.

A year before, as a proselyte in Alexandria, Ethan had experienced Sukkot. But celebrating it as an accepted member of the Jewish community, as a ger tzedek in Jerusalem, was something else again. He loved singing the Hallel during the walk up to the holy city. He loved being with his new family and learning the deeper meanings of the observances and celebrations. He loved seeing all the pilgrims crowded into the courts of the temple. He loved sitting with the family in the sukkah and sharing a meal and praising Adonai.

His lone regret was that Dobah couldn't be with him every moment of every day of the festival.

As Ethan and the family headed back to Bethlehem later that morning, Levi demanded—as only a boy his age could—that Ethan and Yosef swing him between them as they walked. Clasping their hands tightly, the little boy squealed with delight as he sailed through the air, up and then back again. Ethan could almost hear Dobah's laughter joining their son's. Oh, how she loved moments like this.

As if reading Ethan's mind, Yosef said, "I miss Miryam and Yeshua too."

"Are my feelings so obvious?"

"Yes. But remember. There will be other years. Dobah will not always be left behind."

"I know."

Yosef's smile vanished. "But she is struggling, I think."

Ethan nodded, not surprised Yosef had noticed the change in Dobah. She was happy…and yet she was not. Machla had told him Dobah was simply tired. It was not easy to carry a baby to term and then to deliver it. He wanted to believe his mother-in-law was right, but he thought Dobah's moodiness had more to do with his arrest.

His incarceration had been brief, not even a full day, but that fact didn't seem to comfort her.

"She is afraid," Yosef said. "And there is a root of bitterness growing inside of her."

Up ahead, Ethan saw several Roman soldiers walking toward them. They were talking and laughing, paying little heed to the other travelers on the road. They walked with entitlement, expecting others to get out of their way in a hurry—which the people did. They parted for the soldiers like the Red Sea had parted before the Hebrews escaping Pharaoh.

It wasn't fear that rose inside Ethan as he watched it all happen. It was anger.

"The Lord has done it this very day; let us rejoice today and be glad."

The words they had sung that morning came back to him, and his breath caught. He knew he would rather rejoice in Adonai than dwell in anger. He wanted no root of bitterness to take hold of him or his wife. He must not let it. Averting his gaze from the soldiers, he asked Yosef, "How do I help her?"

"Why do you ask me?"

"Because you are wise." Lowering his voice slightly, he added, "And you are the only man I know whom Adonai has spoken to through dreams."

"Up!" Levi cried, intruding on the conversation that had slowed his fun. "Up!"

The two men obliged, swinging the boy high in the air.

They continued on, Ethan now silent as he asked Adonai to show him the way.

CHAPTER THIRTY-TWO

Two months later, in the month of Tevet, 3 BC

In obedience to the law, on the eightieth day following the birth of Rachel, Dobah walked to Jerusalem for her purification ceremony, the baby cradled in her arms. On her right, Ethan carried a lamb for the burnt offering. Her parents walked close behind them, her abba bearing Levi on his shoulders.

Dobah hadn't been to Jerusalem since before Rachel's birth, and it felt strange to walk this road after so long a time. Had it felt strange when she came to the temple after Levi's birth? She couldn't remember. She didn't think so. But it did now.

The road wasn't as busy as it was during festival times, but a steady flow of people still traveled to and from the holy city. As they came closer to the southern gate, Roman soldiers were present as well. Some on horseback. Most on foot. At the sight of them, Dobah's heart began to race. She lowered her gaze to the ground even as she moved a little closer to Ethan's side.

"Dobah?" he said softly.

She gave her head a slow shake in answer.

Her husband and parents were worried about her. She knew it, but she didn't know how to reassure him or them. Ever since Sukkot, she had stayed close to home, spending most of her time indoors, out of sight of others. Her walks to the well in Bethlehem were made in haste. She never lingered long to talk with other women of the village. Always she watched for the Romans to come marching in to destroy her life, to take Ethan or Abba or even Levi away. At night, she often dreamed of the soldiers she had seen in Bethlehem. She heard their laughter before... Before what, she didn't know. She always awoke with a scream in her throat, a scream that wouldn't escape but stayed there, choking her.

Despite her downcast gaze, she was aware Ethan was looking behind them, no doubt communicating silently with her abba. Her suspicion was confirmed when Abba and Imma came up beside her on the left and then, with a few swift steps, positioned themselves in front of her. Tears burned her eyes, and for a moment, she thought she might be sick. She pressed her hand against her mouth, swallowing the bile that rose in her throat.

"Dobah," Ethan said again, "are you all right?"

She swallowed again as she lowered her hand. "I am fine." She blinked away the tears and met his gaze. "I am well, Ethan."

His expression said he didn't believe her.

She drew a deep breath and looked forward again, seeing little but her abba's back as they passed through the gates and into the city.

The Lord is my strength and my shield; my heart trusts in Him, and He helps me. My heart leaps for joy, and with my song I praise Him.

As the words played in her mind and heart, she drew in a breath and released it.

The Lord is the strength of His people, a fortress of salvation for His anointed one. Save Your people and bless Your inheritance; be their shepherd and carry them forever.

She breathed deeply a second time and turned the song into a silent prayer and declaration of faith.

The Lord is my strength and my shield; my heart trusts in Him, and He helps me. My heart leaps for joy, and with my song I praise Him. The Lord is the strength of His people, a fortress of salvation for His anointed one. Save Your people and bless Your inheritance; be their shepherd and carry them on forever.

She repeated the prayer as they moved closer to the temple, the streets growing more crowded. The breeze brought the scent of smoke from the sacrifices being made.

Create in me a pure heart, O God, and renew a steadfast spirit within me.

She lifted her eyes to the wide expanse of blue above them. She wanted to be steadfast, unwavering. She wanted her heart to be clean.

Help me, Adonai. You are my only hope.

Night arrived early in the month of Tevet. Oil lamps flickered as Dobah and her imma cleared away the last remnants of the evening meal. When all was once again in order, Dobah took Levi upstairs and sat beside him until he fell asleep. That didn't take long. It had been a full day for all of them but especially for her little boy.

Before leaving the room, she checked on Rachel to see that the baby girl was sleeping as soundly as her brother. Then she went down the stairs again. A glance from Abba told her Ethan was outside. She went to the door and looked for him. Her husband sat on a small bench, his back leaning against the wall of the house.

Despite the dark of the moonless night, he saw her too. "Come. Join me."

She moved to do so, and after she'd settled at his side, Ethan put his arm around her shoulders, drawing her close. She was glad for the warmth of his body. The night air was cool.

"Every time I experience another ceremony in the temple," Ethan said, his voice soft, "I am thankful I am allowed to be a part of Adonai's chosen people."

Dobah said nothing.

"Look at the heavens, my love. Look at all the stars."

She obeyed. "Beautiful."

"We must not doubt that Adonai, the One who created those heavens, will bring about His will for His people."

Softly, she quoted, "'The Lord is my strength and my shield; my heart trusts in Him, and He helps me. My heart leaps for joy, and with my song I praise Him. The Lord is the strength of His people, a fortress of salvation for his anointed one. Save Your people and bless Your inheritance.'"

"What is that?"

"Another song of King David. I thought of it today as we walked to Jerusalem."

"'Save Your people'" Ethan repeated in a whisper, "'and bless Your inheritance.'"

"It is what you said too. That God will bring about His will for His people. He will save us and bless His inheritance."

Ethan kissed the top of her head. "And do you believe it?"

She wanted to answer in the affirmative. Honesty demanded something else. "Sometimes."

"That is a start."

"But is it enough?" She hadn't meant to ask the question aloud but couldn't take it back once she had.

"Faith was credited to Abraham as righteousness."

"My faith is so small."

He kissed her head again. "Is not a little faith still faith?"

Dobah didn't know the answer to his question. She hoped one day she would.

CHAPTER THIRTY-THREE

Pruning, Ethan's father-in-law told him, was one of the most critical vineyard tasks in winter. Along with other workers, Boaz and Ethan prepared the vines for the next season by cutting away unneeded growth, while a few men repaired any damaged wood and stone trellises.

"The grapes require good airflow and exposure to the sunlight," Boaz explained as he cut away a small section of vine. "The work we do now will benefit us all next year."

Over the past ten months, Ethan had found Boaz to be a patient teacher, perhaps even more patient than Yosef had been in Alexandria. Ethan had learned he liked working in the vineyard even more than he had liked working with stone and wood. Perhaps it was being outdoors that appealed to him. He'd spent his life riding and sleeping beneath an open sky. He felt at home in the vineyard as he hadn't in the large city.

"You are good for her, you know," Boaz said, intruding on Ethan's thoughts.

"Sorry?" He looked at his father-in-law.

"You are good for Dobah. I do not mean you are good to her. That has always been true, even when you barely knew her. No, you are good *for* her. She trusts you. She listens to you. She will find her way again."

"Ever since my arrest..." He let his words trail into silence, knowing they weren't necessary.

"Perhaps you should take her away for a while."

"Take her away?"

Boaz sat back on his haunches. "Machla has a relative in Bethsaida. Perhaps a few weeks near the Sea of Galilee would restore Dobah."

A flock of birds flew over their heads, and Ethan looked up to watch them as they swirled with precision before disappearing beyond some trees at the far end of the vineyard.

He thought of Dobah as she'd been when he first met her. A young widow with a young son, she had suffered a tragic loss with the death of her husband. But she hadn't let sorrow keep her captive. She had been afraid on the night Herod's soldiers came to Bethlehem, but it had been fear of the moment, not fear of the future. She'd been brave, despite the circumstances. She had made the long journey to Egypt without complaint. She had married him and made a new life for herself in a strange city in a strange land. Together, they had studied the Scriptures, looking to understand the messianic prophecies.

Why was she so gripped by anxiety now? Ethan's injuries on the day of his arrest had healed, and his incarceration had been less than a full day, thanks to Boaz's intervention. It could have been so much worse than it was. Why did the memory still hold Dobah in fear over two months later? He thought of the days of travel it would take to reach Bethsaida. They would be on roads where they might come upon more Roman soldiers. Perhaps such a trip would only make things worse.

"Would going to Bethsaida really help her?" Ethan asked aloud.

"I do not know, but it might. I pray it will." Boaz was silent for a short while, and then he gave a firm nod. "Yes, I think you should take Dobah and the children away from Bethlehem. Go, Ethan, with my blessing."

Dobah was in the upper room, nursing Rachel, when the men returned from the vineyard. At the sound of their voices, she breathed a sigh of relief. Ethan and Abba were home again. They were safe for another night.

When her daughter's hunger was sated, Dobah placed the sleeping infant into the larger basket that now served as her bed and walked to the door of the kataluma. As she pulled it open, she heard Imma ask, "When will you leave?"

Dobah's heart started to race. Where was Ethan going? Or Abba? Or both?

"In a few days," Ethan answered.

Dobah stepped through the doorway, pausing on the landing to look down at her parents, husband, and son, all of them clustered near the table, Levi riding on Abba's shoulders as he loved to do. She must have made some sound, for they all turned to look up at her.

"Where are you going?" she asked, a tremor in her voice.

"Bethsaida."

"Why?" Her hand sliding along the wall on her right, she descended the steps.

"So you can visit your aunt," Abba answered.

The fearful pounding of her heart began to ease. "I am going to see Keziah?"

"We are." Ethan stepped toward her. "You, me, and the children. All of us."

Legs unsteady beneath her, Dobah sank onto a nearby stool.

Imma came to sit next to her. "My sister will find great joy in spending time with Levi and Rachel. You know how she is with the little ones." Imma sent a look toward Abba.

He nodded. "Keziah has not been to Jerusalem since soon after Levi was born. She will love to see how he has grown."

Dobah's gaze alternated between her parents. "Is she expecting us?"

"No," Imma answered, "but she has always said to come to see her anytime. She will be happy to have you accept her invitation."

Dobah knew what they were doing, of course. Just like yesterday as they'd approached Jerusalem, her parents were joining with Ethan to help her, to protect her. It made her thankful, sad, and angry, all at the same time. She didn't want to be this way. She didn't want to feel this fragile.

Drawing a breath, she thought back to the months when she, at the age of twelve, had stayed with her aunt in Bethsaida. Uncle Asher had died, and her childless aunt was alone and needed company. Dobah's parents had agreed to allow their youngest daughter to stay with Keziah for a time. The area around the Sea of Galilee was so different from the hill country surrounding Bethlehem, and she had loved it there. She'd loved being able to walk down to the water and watch the fishermen setting off in their boats. She'd loved the way the air smelled, even the fishy smells. Remembering it brought a smile to her lips.

"Yes," she whispered. "I would like to go to Bethsaida."

CHAPTER THIRTY-FOUR

It was strange how natural it felt to Dobah as she walked beside Ethan while he led the donkey, or when she sat with the children in the bumpy cart or as she cooked a meal over a campfire in the evenings. She had longed for Bethlehem after they left Alexandria, but perhaps she'd been born for the life of a nomad. Ethan had lived that way most of his life, back when his name had been Menes.

Throughout the journey to Bethsaida, Dobah found her spirits lifting a little more each day. And on the final day, her excitement grew as she recognized more and more of the surroundings. When Capernaum was behind them, she felt the urge to run ahead of her husband and children, the way she'd run along this same road as a girl of twelve.

"How long ago was it that you stayed with your aunt?" Ethan asked, perhaps as a way of keeping her beside him.

"Almost ten years." She gazed at the lake on her right, fishing boats bobbing in the distance, her excitement turning to wonder. "So much has happened in that time. I grew from a girl to a woman. I was married and widowed. I lived in Egypt and married again. I have borne a son and a daughter. I feel so very different from the girl I was, but nothing here seems to have changed."

"And your aunt. When did you see her last?"

Star of Wonder: Dobah's Story

Dobah felt quite certain he knew already, but she indulged him. "Not yet three years ago. Levi was an infant when she came to Jerusalem for Pesach. Most years she cannot make the trip. It is too far for her to walk. But neighbors were able to bring her in a wagon that year."

"You are close to her?"

Dobah smiled. "I love Keziah, but she can be difficult. Imma calls her stubborn, and I suppose it is true. She does like things her own way."

"Do you think she will be glad to have family descend upon her?" For the first time, there was uncertainty in his eyes.

"She will be glad. She loves to be with children. Perhaps because she had none of her own. The months I stayed with her, she often tended the children of her neighbors while they baked or shopped or cleaned." Dobah laughed softly. "She will tolerate you and me so she can have Levi and Rachel in her home."

Ethan didn't look convinced.

Dobah might have fallen into doubt as well, if the memories of Keziah with Levi weren't so clear in her mind. Her aunt had longed for children. Was she barren, or would she have become pregnant if not for Uncle Asher's lengthy illness and eventual death? Others thought it some consolation Keziah had not been left impoverished, as was true of so many widows in Israel. Asher had seen to it that his widow could live out her life in modest comfort, even if she chose never to marry again.

And why hadn't Keziah married again? Dobah frowned at the question. Her aunt was pretty. Perhaps Adonai would have blessed her with a long-desired child if she'd married a second time.

In the distance, just as the road began to bend to the right, she saw one of the homes on the edge of the village. "We are almost there." She reached for Ethan's free hand. "Let's hurry."

Even as she quickened her footsteps, she looked back at the cart. Levi still slept soundly, curled on his left side, but Rachel, lying in her basket, stared up at the sky with wide eyes, as if seeing something amazing.

Keziah's welcome was exactly what Dobah expected it would be. But though her aunt was truly glad to see Dobah again and to meet Ethan for the first time, it was obvious which members of the family were the favored ones. It wasn't long after their arrival before Rachel slept in the crook of her great-aunt's arm, and Levi—while often shy around people he didn't know—sat on her knee.

"The last time I saw you," Keziah said to the little boy, "you were not much bigger than your sister." She leaned toward him and lowered her voice. "Do you remember when you were that little?"

Eyes large, Levi shook his head, as if he fully understood the question.

Ethan put a hand on Dobah's shoulder. "I will see to the donkey while you two visit."

As soon as he was out the door, Keziah said, "Your husband is giving us time alone." There was a sparkle in her dark eyes when she asked, "How did the two of you meet?"

Dobah thought back to the day the magi came to their door in Bethlehem. What would Keziah think of that story? Was it even her story to tell? Herod himself had threatened Yeshua's life because the baby had been called the King of the Jews. Better to be cautious while still telling the truth. If she could manage it.

"Ethan was a visitor to Bethlehem. He...he worked for Abba for a short while, but he had spent his life working in caravans, transporting goods along the trade routes. A khabir, most sought after." She drew in a slow breath. "He was present in our home on the night the king's soldiers came to Bethlehem to kill the young boys and infants. He helped me escape with Levi."

The smile faded from her aunt's face. "No wonder you love him."

"It is not the reason I love him. At least, not the only reason. Ethan is kind and brave and wise. Adonai blessed me when I became his wife."

Keziah nodded. "I can see that."

Levi slid off his great-aunt's knee and scurried over to Dobah.

"Now tell me why I am honored by this visit. Is my sister well? Is Boaz?"

"My parents are both well." She ran a hand over her son's hair. "They know how much I loved the time I spent with you when I was young, and they thought it would be good for me to visit you again. I...I have not slept well in recent weeks. I have been...anxious. They believe a few weeks by the Sea of Galilee will be good for me. For all of us. And I wanted you to meet Ethan and Rachel and see how much Levi has grown."

Her aunt looked skeptical, but Dobah chose silence as she turned her attention to her son.

CHAPTER THIRTY-FIVE

Several days later, Ethan sank onto the ground, unnoticed by his wife and son as they waded at the edge of the lake. He heard Levi's high-pitched giggle of delight as water splashed higher on his legs. He considered joining them, but first he wanted to take in the sight of Dobah's smiling profile. He'd hoped, of course, that coming to Galilee would bring about a change in her. That it would drive out the fear that had plagued her over these past couple of months. And now it seemed their visit was accomplishing just that. Dobah looked carefree, and it made her all the more beautiful in his eyes.

A breeze caught at her scarf, causing it to slip to her shoulders. She let go of Levi's hand long enough to cover her hair with the fabric again, and the boy bounded away from her, splashing and laughing. Dobah laughed too as she hurried after him, and the sound drew Ethan to his feet.

"Aren't you cold?" he called down to her as he walked to the water's edge.

Dobah faced him, her smile blossoming even more. "Yes, I am. It is not warm enough to play in the water." She gave an exaggerated shiver. "But I could not tell Levi no when he wanted to go wading."

"You spoil the boy."

She stepped from the water, stopping before him. "And you spoil me."

"Do I, beloved?"

"Yes." She caressed his cheek with one hand. "You do."

"You are happy here."

"I am happy wherever you are."

"Not entirely true."

A slight frown creased her forehead, and he leaned close to kiss it.

"It was not *because* of you that I was not happy," she said. "But I was so afraid *for* you. I was afraid for Imma and Abba and for our children."

"And now?"

Her frown deepened before she answered. "I am still afraid, I think. Sometimes. But I am not cowering any longer. Does that make sense?"

"I am not sure." He hesitated then added, "There are Romans patrolling these roads too. They still rule the people of Israel."

"That is true."

Levi tugged on Ethan's tunic, and Ethan quickly lifted the boy into his arms while keeping his eyes locked with Dobah's.

A wistful smile curved the corners of her mouth. "'The name of the Lord is a fortified tower; the righteous run to it and are safe.'" She paused then added, "I am trying to remember those words whenever the need arises."

During his life with the caravans, Ethan had faced many dangers. Dangers in nature including sandstorms, poisonous snakes, and wild beasts. Dangers from bandits intent on killing and stealing. He had fought back against the dangers that came his way, despite whatever fear he'd felt, and he had survived by the skills he'd learned. But he hadn't known Adonai then. He hadn't known he could take shelter in His name. Now he knew, and he was grateful his wife knew it too. They would teach this truth to their son and daughter and to other children if they were blessed with them. They would trust in Adonai, no matter what.

He shifted Levi to his side before pressing his forehead against Dobah's and saying, "'Where does my help come from? My help comes from the Lord, the Maker of heaven and earth.'"

They were still for a long while, neither of them speaking. But then Levi protested the inactivity. Ethan took a reluctant step backward.

"We should return to the house," Dobah said. "Rachel will be hungry soon."

He reached for her hand, and they began walking toward the village.

"Your husband," Keziah said softly one afternoon, "does not like to be idle."

Dobah looked toward the connected stable where Ethan was working on a ladder. He'd replaced a few broken rungs and set them with wooden pegs. Now he secured them with strips of leather. Unlike the stable at home, this one was on the same level as the main room of the house, making it easy to see Ethan, the ladder, and the goat as it munched on some feed in the manger.

"He has repaired everything he can in my little home," her aunt continued. "Soon he will have to go looking for things that are broken. Perhaps he will ask my neighbors what he can do for them."

"Are you saying it is time for us to return to Bethlehem, Keziah? Are we in the way?"

"No. I would have you stay forever if I could keep you. But Boaz will not want to spare Ethan for long from the vineyard, and my sister will not want to miss seeing her grandchildren grow."

Ethan looked up from the ladder and stared through the slats of wood that separated the stable from the living quarters. "We will stay another week." A grin tugged at the corners of his mouth. "There are still a few repairs I can make on the roof before I begin troubling your neighbors."

"There is nothing wrong with your hearing," Keziah said with a cock of her eyebrow.

Dobah laughed as she lowered her gaze to the tunic in her lap and slipped the needle made of bone into the fabric, repairing a small tear. A short while later, she realized a deep frown had creased her brow. She glanced up and realized why. The room had grown dark. Just then, a gust of wind rattled the house.

Ethan went to the door. "A storm is brewing. I will close the shutters." He opened the door and went outside.

"The storms come so suddenly this time of year." Keziah brought an oil lamp to set on the table next to Dobah. "It will be dangerous on the lake." The temperature in the room grew noticeably cooler, and after lighting two more oil lamps, Keziah pulled her chair closer to the fire on the hearth.

Outside, Ethan closed and latched the shutters over the narrow window openings, increasing the darkness of the interior. By the time her husband reentered the house, the wind no longer gusted. Instead, it roared, coming through the hills in the east on its way to the Sea of Galilee. The goat bleated its objection to the sound, and Levi climbed onto Dobah's lap, forcing her to set aside her sewing.

"I have been in storms like this." Ethan sat on a cushion beside Rachel's basket where she slept peacefully. "But those were in the desert where the sand can bury a village before the wind dies down."

"What did you do?" Keziah asked. "How did you survive?"

"The key was to be aware, to watch the sky for signs of a storm and to take action before it arrived. When we saw signs, we sought shelter. Rock formations or even sand dunes could be enough. But if they were not available, we would pitch tents with the openings away from the wind, anchoring them down so they would not blow away. The most important thing was to protect our noses and mouths so we were not inhaling the sand. We had to do the same for the camels. Sandstorms can last not just for hours but for days, so we made sure all the men stayed together, and we rationed both food and water while we waited it out."

Keziah's eyes were wide, much as Dobah's had been the first time she'd heard tales such as this. "Did that happen to you often?" her aunt asked.

"No." Ethan chuckled softly. "Not often. Caravans mostly travel during the times of year when sandstorms are less frequent, and a wise khabir avoids the peak sandstorm season altogether. I was fortunate to learn from a wise khabir."

Dobah placed her hand on his shoulder. "And you became a wise khabir yourself."

"Do you miss it? Traveling with the caravans."

"No, Keziah, I do not. I thought I might because it was all I had known since I was a small boy." His gaze captured Dobah's in the flickering light of the oil lamp. "But I do not. I am content with life in Bethlehem. I have learned much from Boaz, and I still have more to learn from him. The work in the vineyard interests me."

Keziah put her hands on the table and tried to wiggle it. "You must have learned much from Yosef as well. My table was unsteady until you came to visit."

As the noise of the wind outside intensified, Dobah imagined herself in the desert, without the benefit of a sturdy house built of stones to protect her from a sandstorm. She thanked Adonai she hadn't had to face anything like that during their escape to Egypt nor the return trip to Israel almost a year later.

Rain began to splatter against the house. Dobah wondered about the fishermen who had been out on the lake that afternoon. Had they seen the storm coming? Had there been time to row ashore before it arrived? Sometimes life was like this storm, she thought. Trouble blew in, unexpected. One needed to be alert to the signs, to be prepared for what would come.

"*The name of the Lord is a fortified tower; the righteous run to it and are safe.*"

CHAPTER THIRTY-SIX

Not all of the fishermen had seen the warning in the sky. Not all had managed to row ashore before the storm arrived. News of a missing boat and its local crew arrived at Keziah's door early the next morning. Ethan quickly joined with others to go look for survivors.

Holding Rachel in her arms, Dobah watched her husband as he hurried toward the lake. She wasn't surprised he'd answered the call for help, but it did concern her that he was a poor swimmer. He'd admitted it to her once when they were in Alexandria. It hadn't seemed important to her then. When would he have cause to venture out on the sea? But now he was volunteering to go on a boat. Couldn't another storm blow in as quickly as yesterday?

She gave her head a slight shake, refusing to allow her thoughts to turn to fear. Ethan was strong. He would be good with the oars. He was wise. He would know what to do and how to act, even on a fishing boat.

The hours passed at a snail's pace, despite the work filling her day. Dobah milked the goat. She washed clothes and ground grain and swept the floor. She made a second trip to the communal well for more water and made preparations for the evening meal. She nursed Rachel and listened to Levi jabber in his own peculiar language. More than once she went to the door and looked toward the Sea of Galilee, hoping to see her husband returning home.

And finally, she did see him. Her pulse leaped with excitement then nearly stopped when she realized the man walking beside him was a Roman soldier.

"The name of the Lord is a fortified tower... The name of the Lord is a fortified tower... The name of the Lord is a fortified tower."

The two men stopped in the road—still some distance away. They clasped wrists and stared into each other's eyes as they said a few words, and finally the Roman turned on his heel and strode away. Ethan watched the other man for a while before continuing on his way to Keziah's home. He must have been lost in thought because he was nearly to the house before he noticed Dobah standing in the doorway. A concerned expression flashed across his face, but he didn't allow it to linger.

"We found them," he said, giving her a tentative smile. "All the men are safe and well. They spent the night in Capernaum because the boat was damaged as they came ashore in the storm."

Looking beyond Ethan's shoulder, Dobah saw a few other men walking up the road to the village. She wondered if they had delayed their return because of the Roman who had been with her husband. Perhaps reading her mind, Ethan turned to look.

"I knew him as a boy," he said.

"Who?"

"Atticus Barba. The soldier."

Confused, she gave a slow shake of her head as he met her gaze again.

"Atticus traveled on one of the caravans with his merchant father. I was assigned to look after him, to keep him safe during the journey. I was older by a couple of years, and he looked up to me."

"How...? Where...?"

"His auxiliary century is stationed in Capernaum. We met by chance on the shore. Believe it or not, he recognized me, even after all these years." Ethan's expression confirmed his surprise. "I did not know him at first. Not until he called me Menes. There was something about his voice, I think. Then I saw in his eyes the boy he used to be."

"He is a Roman."

"He is not a citizen of Rome."

"Does that make a difference? He is one of their soldiers. He is part of the army that suppresses Israel. He follows the orders of their commanders." She took a step back, a hand on her breastbone. "He is the same as the men who arrested you, who beat you, who put you in prison."

Ethan glanced over his shoulder one more time before entering the house. "He is not the same, Dobah."

"How do you know he is different? You said you were boys when you knew each other." Anger roiled in her chest. "How do you know what type of man he has become after so many years?"

Ethan reached out, placing both of his hands on her shoulders, silently urging her to meet his gaze. "Perhaps I do not know this moment. But I would like to get to know in the few remaining days we are in Bethsaida."

"Did we not come here so I can forget the soldiers?"

He didn't answer, simply watched her.

With a huff of air, she turned her back to him and went to the pot hanging over the fire. Her thoughts churned as she stirred the stew. She and Ethan had been married more than a year, and in that time, she'd never felt anger toward him. Irritation, perhaps. Frustration, definitely. But true anger? Never. Not until now. How could he not see that associating with a Roman soldier wasn't acceptable? Not to her. Not to other Jews.

In the days that followed Ethan's unexpected meeting with Atticus Barba, he twice absented himself from Keziah's home, staying away for hours both times. Dobah didn't ask him where he'd gone or who he'd seen while he was away. She had her suspicions and didn't want them confirmed. By the day of their departure for their return trip to Bethlehem, Dobah was barely speaking to him. If he noticed, he didn't show it. Which only served to irritate her more.

It was still early morning when Dobah hugged Keziah farewell while Ethan waited with the children beside the donkey cart.

"You do yourself no favor," her aunt said softly as she drew back to look Dobah in the eyes. "Ethan is a good man. A loyal man. Loyal to you and loyal to his friends. You would not have him be otherwise."

"He does not understand why this upsets me."

"He understands more than you do, Dobah." Her aunt hesitated before adding, "Stubbornness does not prove you are right."

The comment stung. "I am *not* stubborn."

Keziah shook her head. "You have a long journey ahead of you, dear one. Use it to make peace with your husband."

"But—"

"Is your silence bringing you two together? Is it bringing you happiness?"

"Well, no, but—"

"I have been stubborn in my life, and it did not improve anything. I will pray for you. And I will pray for a safe and productive journey back to Bethlehem." Keziah hugged her again. "Who knows? Perhaps I will be able to join your family at Pesach this year."

Dobah knew better than to argue further. "Imma and Abba would love it if you could come to stay. So would I." She turned away, looking toward Ethan. Her aunt was right. She had been stubborn, and it served no purpose. Only how could she make the anger go away?

Ethan let his wife's silence continue throughout their first day of travel. But after their evening meal was eaten and the children had fallen asleep, he knew he couldn't allow it to go on any longer.

"Dobah, sit with me."

She glanced toward the tent, its flap open to the breeze off the lake, as if wanting to escape inside of it. But she lowered herself to a pillow on the ground instead.

"We need to talk about it," he said.

"About what?"

A smile tugged at the corners of his mouth, but he fought against it. It would only fuel her anger if she thought he was amused by her. "About my friendship with Atticus."

"Your friendship with an enemy of our people."

"He is not my enemy, Dobah. And he has made other friends among the Jews in Capernaum. Remember. His people were conquered by the Romans as well."

"Then why did he become one of their soldiers?"

"We do not always have the freedom to choose. You know that."

Dobah looked off toward the Sea of Galilee, her face hidden in shadows. "You met with him more than once since the storm."

"I did. I wanted to know about him, why he left his father's trade, how long he's been in Israel, if he had a family."

"But you never brought him to Keziah's."

"Would you have welcomed him?"

She was silent awhile before answering. "No."

Ethan reached over and enveloped her hand in his. "I was once a man without faith. I believed in nothing beyond my own wisdom. But that changed as I listened to the magi on our trek from the East. Then I found myself in the presence of the Messiah, the newborn King of the Jews, and my life was altered forever." He squeezed her fingers. "Do you not think the same could happen to Atticus, if he were given the chance?"

"You were never a Roman. He is."

"I was a man who lived in ignorance of the Living God. Is Atticus any different?"

Dobah released a breath, and he sensed the stiffness going out of her.

"Perhaps one day I will see Atticus again, and he too will have become a righteous convert."

This elicited a sound of disbelief from her.

Ethan released her hand then put an arm around her shoulders and drew her close to his side. "Is anything too hard for Adonai?"

"No," she whispered.

They were silent for a long while, but it was a better kind of silence than before.

At last Dobah said, "I am sorry, Ethan. I was not right to behave as I did. You did not deserve to be treated that way."

"Ah, beloved." He kissed her cheek. "It is well between us. That is all that matters now."

She placed her head on his shoulder then. "Nothing is too hard for Adonai."

CHAPTER THIRTY-SEVEN

Ten years later, in the month of Nisan, 9 AD

Dobah paused on the road leading to her abba's vineyard and turned her face toward the sky, allowing the gentle warmth of the sun to caress her face.

The winter season had seemed long, and she was thankful for all the signs of spring. The green hillsides were covered in blankets of red, pink, white, and purple wildflowers. Lambs and kids cavorted as shepherds watched their flocks. The barley crops were nearing harvesttime while the fields of wheat were maturing. At the vineyard, Ethan, Abba, and Levi worked to prepare the soil around the vines, removing weeds and aerating the ground, readying the grapevines for a new growing season.

From her girlhood, spring had been Dobah's favorite season. The colors of the sky and the earth, the freshness of the air, the mild temperatures, the baby animals being born. Everything about the season seemed to fill her with hope. And she needed that feeling this year more than ever.

Imma had fallen ill before the end of the previous summer, passing away a few months later. Not long after Imma's death, Noah—the second of Dobah's three sons—had fallen while climbing a steep hillside and broken his leg. Although he could walk without a crutch, he did so with a limp. To make life even more difficult, the vineyard's wine sales had dropped at the same time taxes had been raised by the Romans.

"Send spring into my heart, Adonai," she whispered before continuing on her way.

It was three days until the beginning of Pesach. Meal preparations in her abba's house were well underway. As was true every year, they'd made room for guests, unsure how many relatives or friends would show up at their door, looking for their hospitality. But whoever came would be welcome.

As she reached the top of the next rise, the vineyard came into view. Dobah saw workers kneeling between the rows, the sun upon their backs, their cloaks laid aside as the day warmed. It took only a glance to identify her eldest son working near his grandfather.

In the past few months, Levi had shot up several inches, and his voice had deepened. Both changes made it easier for him to fit in with the older boys in Bethlehem. Everyone knew, of course, that Levi was the only male of thirteen years in the village, and they knew the reason why. It made him special. It made him stand out, especially on the anniversary of that dreadful night.

A quiet, thoughtful boy and not one to invite attention, Levi had been glad when he could leave the Beth Talmud and go to work with his abba and grandfather in the vineyard. He'd always been a good student and had memorized the Shema and the Hallel at an early age. He'd studied the written Torah in Beth Sefer and then the oral Torah while attending Beth Talmud. He'd learned the art of asking good questions of his teachers. Perhaps, if not for his unique status in the village, he would have continued in the Beth Midrash. Perhaps he would have learned the art of debating with his teachers. Perhaps he would have done well enough to one day become a *talmid* under a rabbi of authority. That honor would have made any parent proud. But such was not Levi's wish. He wanted to be ordinary. He wanted to be like other boys in Bethlehem rather than to be the one who had survived the slaughter of the innocents.

As she left the road, Abba straightened and saw her. "Dobah, what brings you here at this hour?" He looked up at the sun, as if to confirm the time of day.

"Yiska is visiting with Savta. It gave me an opportunity to bring you some fresh bread." Dobah held out the loaf wrapped in a cloth.

"And to walk in the hills, see the flowers, and breathe the spring air."

"You know me well, Abba."

He smiled. "I know you well."

It wasn't often Dobah had the freedom to walk for pleasure. She walked to the well for water. She walked to the market stalls to buy grain and oil and fruit. But walking for pleasure? No. The demands made by a large family—cooking, cleaning, washing clothes—kept Dobah close to their home most of the time. Not to mention how frail her grandmother had become this past year.

Abba looked over his shoulder. "Ethan! Levi! Come join us."

Levi arrived first, and after a brief smile in Dobah's direction, his gaze settled on the bread. Like any fast-growing boy his age, he was always hungry.

"Take it," Abba said to Levi. "But share it."

Levi did as he was told, breaking off a piece for himself before handing the loaf to Ethan, who had arrived by that time.

"Have we any guests yet?" her husband asked.

"Not yet, but Bethlehem's streets are busy as is the road up to Jerusalem."

"Ethan," Abba said, "walk your wife home. Our work here is nearly finished. Levi and I will be along soon."

Her husband grinned his thanks, and they started off together. As they climbed the rise in the road, Ethan reached for her hand, and she felt that familiar skip in her heart. Despite more than eleven years of marriage, not to mention the five children she'd borne to him, Ethan could still make her feel like a girl in the flush of first love. All it took was a certain glance or tender touch.

"I remembered something this morning," he said as he squeezed her fingers.

"What was that?"

"This is our thirteenth Pesach together."

"Thirteen?"

"The first came while we were on the road to Egypt. Not long before we reached Alexandria, as I recall."

She thought about it a moment. She had remembered Pesach, of course, during their Shabbat rest in Egypt, but she had done so as a fugitive from Bethlehem. There had been no Pesach meal, no sacrifice in the temple, no way of marking the special occasion with her family. But by the following Pesach, she had been back in Bethlehem with Abba and Imma, no longer a widow but once again a wife.

She looked over at Ethan. He was both different from and the same as the man who had taken her and Levi to safety on that terrifying night. Older, of course, but also wise and kind, strong and quick. Knowledgeable in the Torah as well as the oral law. An honored ger tzedek who was able to debate with rabbis. When he'd led her into the darkness all those years ago, she couldn't have imagined this man who walked beside her now.

He grinned at her. "What are you thinking?"

"How glad I am Adonai brought you to Bethlehem with the magi."

Ethan tugged on her arm, bringing her closer to his side so he could kiss her.

On the following day, Ethan and Levi remained at home to help Dobah with last-moment preparations for Pesach. In the afternoon, Ethan climbed the ladder to the rooftop, where he set about making repairs. He'd discovered a leak the last time it rained, but he'd put off patching it until today.

When the repairs were complete, he straightened from his task, a hand on the small of his back. Looking out over the village, he saw three people walking toward the house. Since there were many visitors to Bethlehem because of the coming festival, they shouldn't stand out. Still, he knew them at once.

"Yosef!" He moved to the raised edge of the rooftop. "Dobah, Yosef is here, and Miryam and Yeshua are with him."

The couple and their oldest son waved at him, and he waved back. An instant later, Dobah appeared from the doorway below and ran to greet her cousin and his family. Levi followed right behind her.

From his vantage point, Ethan watched the hugging and kissing and exchange of greetings before everyone started toward the house.

His gaze settled on the two boys who led the way. Levi at thirteen and Yeshua at twelve were not quite equal in height, but they were alike in many other ways, especially their facial features and lanky builds. He'd heard often that Levi took after his maternal great-grandfather, David. Yeshua did the same. The two boys could have been brothers rather than cousins.

Ethan waited until everyone disappeared into the house then climbed down the ladder and went inside. The three youngest of his children were chasing one another, hiding behind people and chairs, dropping onto cushions, giggling and squealing. Dobah's savta laughed even as she covered her ears with her hands.

"It is good to see you again." Ethan clasped wrists with Yosef. "The other children did not come with you again this year."

"It is a long journey. It will be a few more years before Yeshua's brothers are ready to join us for Pesach."

"Yeshua is growing as fast as Levi."

"Indeed. He will be taller than me one day. I am sure of it."

"Is He learning the trade in your workshop?"

"He joins me when He is not studying. But His studies are what matter most. To Him and to us. Sometimes I wonder what I have to teach Him. There are days when I am convinced I am the student."

"I doubt that is true."

Yosef shook his head. "I am serious, Ethan. I do not always understand the things He says, even when I know He speaks the truth. When He asks questions, it is often done to make others think more than for Him to obtain information. He is…different from other boys His age."

"We already knew that." Ethan glanced around and found Yeshua and Levi seated on the stairs, deep in conversation. "But when will others know?"

"And what will it mean when they do?"

Ethan looked at Yosef again. "It will mean freedom from the Romans, surely. Isn't that what everyone expects?"

Yosef was silent a long while before answering, "I do not think the Messiah's rule will be what is expected."

Something in his friend's expression kept Ethan from asking what he meant by those words. How would the Messiah's rule be different from expectations? For the second time, his gaze moved to the stairs and the two boys sitting there. His chest tightened. A shadow of dread seemed to darken the room, and he wondered what would happen to Yeshua and Levi in the years to come.

While Miryam visited with Savta, Dobah thought about the stew they would eat for supper. She'd need to add more vegetables to the pot if she wanted it to stretch to feed three more people. Thankfully, she'd baked extra bread earlier that day.

"How may I help?" Miryam asked, breaking into Dobah's thoughts.

"I should fetch more water."

"I will come with you." Miryam patted Savta's hand. "We will not be long."

"Do not worry about me," Savta replied with a wave. "It is good to have the family here. You should send Levi to get Boaz."

"Good idea, Savta. I will do that right now."

A short while later, Levi and Yeshua darted out the door on their way to the vineyard. Dobah and Miryam soon left the house at a more sedate pace, their destination the community well. Each carried an empty water jar.

"It is good to see Yeshua again," Dobah said. "It's been eleven years since He last came to Bethlehem."

Miryam nodded. "It is hard to make such a journey with one little one. Much harder as the family grows. It was better for Yeshua to remain in Nazareth while Yosef attended the festivals. But He is twelve now. He does not remember his first Pesach in Jerusalem, but He will remember this one."

"I forget how fortunate I am, how fortunate our children are, to live within an easy walking distance of the temple, especially during the different feasts."

"Yosef is always glad to spend the pilgrim festivals with all of you. There are times I wish we lived in Bethlehem." Her eyes lifted in the direction of Jerusalem. "But we are better off where we are. Yosef does a lot of work in Sepphoris, and Nazareth is home to us."

Dobah set down her jug on a large stone next to the well. "I would have loved raising our children together. And did you see the way Levi and Yeshua were with each other? As if they had spent every Pesach of their lives together."

"I noticed." Miryam smiled. "They are good boys."

"They *are* good boys," Dobah echoed before turning to fill her water jug.

Miryam did the same, and soon they were headed back to the house. On the way, as they walked in comfortable silence, Dobah thought of all that had happened over the years since the birth of Yeshua. So many changes she had never foreseen.

As if reading Dobah's thoughts, Miryam said, "Adonai has blessed us."

"Yes." She troubled her lower lip between her teeth before asking, "Has He... Has Adonai sent another angel to tell you what is to come? Has Yosef had more dreams?"

Miryam shook her head, and she stopped walking, causing Dobah to do the same. "No. We wait and we trust, like all of His people."

"But do you see any...*signs* when you are with Him?"

Miryam's smile was tender. "Yeshua is like other boys...except when He is not."

"I do not understand."

"And I cannot explain it. It is simply something I know." She placed a hand over her heart. "In here."

Perhaps Dobah would see for herself, she thought, during the coming week.

CHAPTER THIRTY-EIGHT

The family sang as they walked up to Jerusalem, on their way to sacrifice the Pesach lamb. Boaz led the group, the unblemished lamb held in his arms.

"'I lift up my eyes to the mountains—where does my help come from? My help comes from the Lord, the Maker of heaven and earth.'"

Dobah carried three-year-old Dinah in her arms. Ahead of her, Rachel held hands with Susannah, who was six. Next to her, Ethan held hands with their younger sons, Noah and Elijah.

"'He will not let your foot to slip—He who watches over you will not slumber; indeed, He who watches over Israel will neither slumber nor sleep.'"

People from Bethlehem—her friends and neighbors—walked ahead of them and behind them, and many joined in the singing.

"'The Lord watches over you—the Lord is your shade at your right hand; the sun will not harm you by day, nor the moon by night.'"

Dobah glanced over her shoulder to see Levi and Yeshua following beside Yosef and Miryam. Behind them were Dobah's sisters and their husbands and children.

"'The Lord will keep you from all harm—he will watch over your life; the Lord will watch over your coming and going both now and forevermore.'"

As they drew closer to Jerusalem, the crowd of pilgrims increased. Near the gate, she saw two Romans on horseback.

Adonai will protect me.

Ethan looked her way, and his eyes seemed to impress those same words upon her heart. She gave him a nod.

Thousands upon thousands of men, in addition to women and children, had come to Jerusalem for the festival of Pesach. They poured into the city, swelling its ranks to about a million souls and filling its inns and guest rooms. Some stayed in tents outside the city or with people in smaller towns beyond the walls of Jerusalem. Special ovens were set up throughout the city for pilgrims to cook their Pesach lambs after the sacrifice, as prescribed by law. Already the air was thick with the scent of roasting meat.

And the level of noise as they drew closer to the temple was overwhelming. People talking and calling out to others. Babies crying and small children shrieking. Lambs bleating and doves in cages cooing. It was like this every festival, but Dobah never grew used to it.

As they drew closer to the temple, her abba stopped and turned to face his family. "Levi. Yeshua. Walk with me the rest of the way. I would share with you."

The boys were quick to obey.

Dobah felt a sting of envy. Abba and Imma had educated her from an early age, and she had attended the Beth Sefer—the House of the Scroll—in the synagogue until she was ten. At that age, girls had to learn to run a proper home. Teaching them was the job of their immas and not a rabbi. After all, many girls would be married by the age of thirteen or fourteen. The boys, the ones who were bright and able, were able to continue for three years in the Beth Talmud—the House of Instruction. But only the brightest and most determined moved on after that in the Beth Midrash—the House of Study. Those were the boys who would one day seek out a teacher of the law and become a disciple.

Levi had not moved on to the Beth Midrash. His formal schooling had come to an end. Her eldest son loved Adonai. He loved the law. He had been a good student and loved to memorize the Scriptures. But he had not excelled in his studies in the way that was required for Beth Midrash students. And he hadn't minded. He loved working beside his abba and saba in the vineyard and seemed content to learn from them.

But Yeshua...

Dobah looked at her cousin's son, and she knew without question that Yeshua would go on to Beth Midrash and most likely that He would become a *talmid* under a rabbi. That He would study and excel in everything set before Him. Was her lack of doubt because she knew His story from the beginning? Or was it the passion for the Most High that was obvious as He stared toward the temple? Perhaps it was both.

The week of Pesach passed in a blur of meals, conversations, and visits to Jerusalem. There was an abundance of worship and laughter. Tears were shed whenever memories of departed loved ones were shared.

On the final morning of their stay in Bethlehem, Yosef and Miryam rose early and left with Yeshua to the place where they were to join a group of pilgrims returning to Galilee. Among them were some of Miryam's cousins as well as neighbors from Nazareth.

Dobah stood in the road, waving farewell until they turned a corner and disappeared from view. Emotions tightened her chest. Oh, how she would miss them. Especially Miryam, who was so precious to her. Closer in many ways than her own sisters.

"We will all miss them," Ethan said behind her.

She turned toward him, tears welling in her eyes. "I feel their going more this year. Perhaps it is because Imma is no longer with us."

"Perhaps."

"How is Levi?"

Ethan put a hand on her shoulder. "We will go to the vineyard and work. That will help."

She offered a wistful smile. It made sense, what her husband said. Work would help all of them forget the sudden absence of those they loved. If Adonai willed it, they would come again next year, and a year was not so very long.

But as it turned out, it wasn't to be a year before she saw Yosef and Miryam again. Instead, on the evening of the next day, her cousin and his wife appeared at their door.

"Is He here?" Miryam asked, panic in her dark eyes.

"Is who here?" Dobah replied.

"Yeshua. Is He here?"

"No." Dobah looked toward Ethan then back at Yosef and Miryam. "He left with you yesterday."

Miryam turned to Yosef and grabbed both of his hands. "Where could He be? It will be dark soon. If He is not here, where could He be?"

Ethan held the door open wide. "Come inside and tell us what has happened."

The couple hesitated a few moments, as if uncertain what to do next. Then, with a nod from Yosef, they stepped into the house.

Abba stood near the head of the table. "The boy is missing?"

"When we made camp last night, we looked for Him." Yosef guided Miryam to a chair and gently urged her to sit on it. "There were many of us traveling together, and we thought He was still with the other boys from Nazareth. But we learned they had not seen Him for many hours. Perhaps not even since we passed by Jerusalem in the morning."

"Did you encounter trouble along the way?" Ethan asked.

"No, the people were many. Too many for thieves to try to steal from us. There was no trouble. Miryam and I left the camp at first light this morning to return to Bethlehem, and we asked everyone we saw along the way if they had seen a boy of twelve all by Himself. No one had. We became convinced He must have returned here." Yosef looked toward the wall near the stairs, where Levi stood. "We were certain he must have come back to see you."

Levi shook his head.

Miryam grasped Yosef's arm. "We must go. We must keep looking."

Abba said, "It will be dark soon, as you said. You would have no hope of finding Him at night. You will stay with us. You will eat something and then sleep. Tomorrow morning, we will all go into Jerusalem. We will help look for Yeshua."

"What if He is not in Jerusalem?" Miryam clasped her hands before her breasts. "What if He is lost?"

Dobah sat on a stool next to Miryam. "Yeshua is God's anointed. He will not be lost."

Tears traced Miryam's cheeks as she silently wept.

Strange, Dobah thought, how certain she felt in that moment. She, who so often was filled with doubt and confusion and fear. But she was certain. Yeshua was not lost. He would be found, and He would be all right.

CHAPTER THIRTY-NINE

Two days of fruitless searching had worn at Dobah's certainty that Yeshua would be found and would be well. Abba, Levi, Ethan, and Dobah searched along with Yosef and Miryam. They walked the streets of Jerusalem and visited every place beyond the walls of the city that might draw a twelve-year-old boy's interest. No one remembered seeing Him.

It was on the third day of their search, as the family entered the temple area once again, that Dobah heard Miryam release a cry of surprise and joy. Dobah followed Miryam's gaze and felt her own jolt of surprise. There was Yeshua, in the Court of the Gentiles, seated among many teachers of the law—identifiable by their clothing. He was listening to the rabbis then speaking. Perhaps in answer to their questions or perhaps asking questions of His own. Beyond the circle of rabbis, men and women stood listening to the exchange.

Yeshua's family moved forward, weaving their way through the people gathered in the court.

"How does a boy His age know such things?" Dobah heard one man ask another. "Who is His teacher? Where did He acquire such knowledge?"

Star of Wonder: Dobah's Story

A woman to Dobah's left said to her husband, "Did you hear how He answered the rabbi's question? Such understanding. I cannot believe it. Our boy could not give such an answer."

Dobah looked at Ethan. Lowering her voice so only he could hear, she said, "It sounds as if Yeshua is teaching the rabbis."

"It sounds that way." A smile tweaked the corners of his mouth.

Once she was close enough to be heard, Miryam softly called, "Yeshua."

He heard her. His eyes flicked in her direction, and He smiled. Then He respectfully excused Himself, stood, and walked toward His parents and other family members.

After embracing Him, Miryam said, "Son, why have You treated us like this? Your abba and I have been anxiously searching for You."

"Why were you searching for Me?" There was a wealth of patience in Yeshua's question. Patience beyond His years. "Did you not know I had to be in my Father's house?"

Miryam and Yosef exchanged confused glances. Dobah did the same with Ethan. His Father's house? What did He mean? Yeshua's home was in Nazareth.

Yosef said, "We journeyed a full day before we discovered You were not with the caravan of pilgrims. We have searched for You for three days."

Yeshua looked from his parents to His other relatives gathered nearby. Then His gaze lifted to the temple, as if in explanation.

"His Father's house," Dobah whispered, her heart fluttering as she spoke the words.

"Come," Abba said. "We will go home. Yeshua, You must be hungry. You will eat, and Your parents will rest, and all of you will be ready to start your journey again in the morning."

Dobah felt many eyes watching them as they once again made their way out of the Court of the Gentiles. She didn't breathe easy until they were beyond the city gates and well on their way back to Bethlehem.

A great fuss was made over Yeshua by Dobah and Ethan's other children. And when they were done, Savta crooked a finger at Yeshua, silently commanding Him to approach her. When He arrived before His great-grandmother, she took His arm and pulled herself up from the chair. Then she placed both hands on His shoulders. Only twelve, He was already a head taller than she was.

"You must never do that to Your imma and abba again, Yeshua ben Yosef. Do You understand me? Honor them that Your days in the land may be prolonged."

"Yes, Savta."

She pressed the palm of one hand against his cheek. "Adonai is always with You. He will guide Your steps."

"'My steps have held to Your paths,'" He answered, His head bowed. "'My feet have not stumbled.'"

"Amen." Savta moved her hand from His cheek to the top of His head. As if giving a blessing.

Dobah's heart fluttered for the second time that day.

That night, in the darkness of the bedchamber, with the youngest children sleeping in their own beds against an opposite wall, Ethan drew Dobah close to his side and softly said, "Yeshua was teaching the teachers."

Ethan had known, from almost the moment he bowed down along with the magi, that Yeshua was special, a promised King. As Ethan had grown in his faith in the Holy God of Israel, as he had studied the Torah and the Nevi'im and the Ketuvim, he had not only believed Yeshua was the promised Messiah but that He was far more than the people of Yahweh expected. Today had only solidified his belief.

Following a lengthy silence, Dobah said, "So many were watching Him and listening to Him. They were marveling at all He knew at His age. I wish…I wish I could have listened to Him for a while."

"I felt the same. Although I am certain I would have reacted the same way Miryam and Yosef did. After not knowing where Yeshua was for days, all they wanted was to have Him back with them."

Dobah nestled closer into the curve of his shoulder and neck. "Yeshua is so much like Levi. They were alike as babies. They are alike as boys. Still, Yeshua is different. He is… He is…" Her voice drifted into silence, perhaps because she couldn't find words to describe Him.

"More," Ethan supplied. "Yeshua is like other boys, but He is also more."

"It is hard for me to understand. He is part of my family. He is the son of my cousin, and yet He is not my cousin's son. How can that be? And why this family? They are so…ordinary. *We* are so ordinary."

Ethan chuckled softly. "You are far from ordinary, Dobah, wife of Ethan and daughter of Boaz."

She turned her head to lightly touch her lips to his collarbone before settling back again. "I *am* your wife and the daughter of Boaz. But I am content to be ordinary. I would not change who I am or who we are. I am content with our ordinary lives."

"As am I." He rested his cheek upon the top of her head, prepared at last to sleep.

CHAPTER FORTY

Dobah spoke the truth on the night Yeshua, a boy of twelve, was found in the temple. She was an ordinary woman, and she lived an ordinary life. She was content with both as the seasons passed, as festivals arrived annually, as she watched her children grow and the other children in her extended family grow. As she saw others age. As she herself aged.

While her savta had always seemed old and frail to Dobah, Savta lived until her eighty-third year. Revered and loved by many in Bethlehem, Dobah's savta was mourned by all. Although she had been tiny, her absence left a large hole in the household.

The year after Savta's death, Boaz followed his imma to the grave. His passing made Dobah an orphan, she realized, and despite her age and the ages of her children, she felt abandoned and alone in a way she could not explain.

Soon after Levi turned eighteen, he became betrothed to the daughter of Bilha and Gershom. The bride's name was Aziel. Dobah thought it a good match, one that would be blessed by Adonai. Over the months following the betrothal, Levi and Ethan added a room onto the house, and soon after its completion, Levi and Aziel married. Yosef and his family came to Bethlehem for the wedding, making it an extra special occasion.

"Will Yeshua take a wife of His own soon?" Dobah asked Miryam during the celebrations that followed.

Miryam shook her head. "He says marriage is not His Abba's will for Him."

Dobah thought it an odd thing to say. Most Jewish men found a bride by the time they were Yeshua's age. But she bit back the questions she wanted to ask, sensing they would not be welcomed.

Rachel was the next of Dobah's children to marry. Her bridegroom lived in Bethany, where his family owned a large olive grove and an olive press. It was an advantageous match. More than that, Rachel adored her new husband, which made it easier for Dobah to see her eldest daughter leave Bethlehem to settle in Bethany.

The next year, word came that Yosef had died. Dobah mourned again, unable to imagine Miryam without Yosef by her side. She wondered about the rest of Yosef's family too. Yeshua, she assumed, would take over His abba's business. His younger brothers probably worked with Him already. His sisters were still too young to marry, so at least Miryam was not entirely alone. But the way the years passed, it wouldn't be long.

The rest of Dobah and Ethan's children became betrothed and married in what seemed quick succession. More rooms were added onto the house, and Noah's and Elijah's brides became a part of the household while their husbands worked with Ethan and Levi in the vineyard. Like their sister Rachel, Susannah and Dinah married young men who didn't live in Bethlehem, but neither moved very far away. Susannah went to Jerusalem and Dinah went to Jericho.

Grandchildren were born. Many of them. One or two every year.

Levi's eldest son, named Boaz after Levi's grandfather, was eleven when rumors came from Galilee about a teacher who had turned water into wine at a wedding in Cana. A rabbi named Yeshua.

It was only the beginning of the stories they would hear in the months to come.

In the month of Nisan, 28 AD

Dobah held tight to Ethan's arm as they moved through the crowds in the city. There were always thousands of pilgrims in Jerusalem during the Pesach festival, but this week something felt different. More tension. Heightened excitement. Something. Over the past few days, she'd heard Yeshua's name spoken time and time again. And even when she hadn't heard His name, she'd heard talk of the Rabbi from Galilee. Today she hoped to see Him for herself.

Miryam had not come to Bethlehem to celebrate Pesach with Dobah and Ethan since before Yosef's death. As for Yeshua and His younger brothers, they had faithfully come to Jerusalem for the pilgrim festivals—just as their abba had done his entire life, except when he lived in Egypt—but none of them had stayed in Bethlehem in recent years. Dobah missed them and tried not to be hurt because they'd chosen to stay elsewhere. Still, Yeshua was a rabbi now. He traveled with His disciples. As for His brothers, they were said to disapprove of Yeshua and His teachings, especially after last year when Yeshua had driven the money changers, along with the sheep and oxen, from the temple.

"Stop making My Father's house a place of business," Yeshua had demanded as He swung a scourge of cords.

Was it any wonder people were looking for Him during Pesach? What would He do this year? What would He say?

Dobah and Ethan had chosen to celebrate the festival in Jerusalem with Rachel and her family. Staying with their daughter meant they didn't have to walk back and forth to Bethlehem throughout the festival. It also meant they could be in Jerusalem on Shabbat, something the walking restrictions prescribed in the law didn't allow them when they slept in their home in Bethlehem. Being in Jerusalem today meant they could look for Yeshua once again.

Her thoughts wandering, Dobah's foot caught on a stone and she stumbled. But Ethan was quick to steady her before she could fall. Even in his mid-fifties, his beard now completely gray, he was as strong as he'd been as a young khabir. "Let's get away from the crowd for a while." He steered her into a less used side street. "Maybe we should return to Rachel's."

"No. I want to see Yeshua. I want to speak to Him."

"We may not find Him in the city today."

"He will be here. I...I cannot explain it, but I'm certain He will. I want to at least try to find Him."

Ethan gave her a patient smile. "All right. But let's not go to the temple yet. Perhaps we will hear from others where He has been seen."

Her husband was right. Not long after, they heard Yeshua had been seen near the Lions' Gate. "Come with me," Ethan said, drawing her along another unfamiliar street.

They didn't try to converse as they made their way. Ethan zigged and zagged from one street to another until they reached their destination. He had just suggested they sit and rest while they watched people coming and going when a woman hurried past them, calling to a friend, "He is at the pool. Hurry. Perhaps the angel will stir the waters."

Dobah's pulse quickened. "It must be Him. Who else would they run for?"

Ethan took her arm once again, and they hurried in the direction of the pool of Bethesda. They were not alone. Others had heard of His presence at the pool too.

Although it had been some years since she'd seen Yeshua, Dobah recognized Him at once. He stood on the opposite side of the pool, near several of the sick who waited for a chance to enter the pool and perhaps be healed. It was said an angel of Adonai came down into the pool at certain seasons. When the waters were stirred by the angel, whoever was first to step into the pool was made well from whatever afflicted them. The blind. The lame. Those with diseases.

Ethan guided Dobah around the edge of the crowd, past one portico then another, until they drew quite close to Yeshua. His back was to them as he knelt beside a man with a paralyzed leg, but she heard Him say, "Do you wish to get well?"

The man answered, "Sir, I have no one to help me into the pool when the water is stirred. While I am trying to get in, someone else goes down ahead of me."

It seemed to Dobah that everyone around the pool had fallen silent, their eyes turned upon Yeshua and the man who could not walk, their ears straining to hear what would be said next.

Yeshua stood and, in a commanding voice, said, "Get up! Pick up your mat and walk."

Dobah held her breath. Perhaps so did everyone.

A confused expression crossed the man's face. Then his eyes went to his leg, a leg that had been misshapen moments before but now looked normal. He touched it with one hand. He bent his knee. He gasped as he looked at Yeshua.

Dobah exchanged a glance with Ethan, who looked as wide-eyed as she felt. What had they witnessed? It was impossible, yet they had seen it for themselves.

The man pushed himself up from the ground, holding a walking stick in one hand. He hopped on what had been his bad leg. He made a sound. Part laugh. Part shout. Then he bent over, picked up his pallet as Yeshua had commanded, and hurried away from the pool.

Yeshua watched the healed man for only a moment before turning away. When He saw Dobah and Ethan, He smiled as He spoke their names. His voice was deep with affection. "Come," He said. "Walk with Me. Tell me how you are. I have missed seeing you."

They fell in beside Him. Several men Dobah didn't know followed behind them. She guessed they must be His disciples, men who sought to become like Yeshua, as all *talmidim* tried to become like their teachers.

"It is Shabbat," Yeshua said. "Are you staying in the city?"

"Yes," Dobah answered. "With Rachel and her husband and children. Could You come back with us to their house? Rachel would love to see You again."

He shook His head. "I am going to the temple now. I must be found there."

Must be found there. Dobah remembered Him as a boy of twelve, found in the temple, talking with the teachers of the law. But things were different now. Yeshua was not an unknown boy from Nazareth, exchanging thoughts with rabbis in the Court of the Gentiles. He was known by many, and His words and deeds were not always appreciated. Especially not in Jerusalem.

"We heard You are staying in Capernaum," Ethan said.

"Much of the time. But I have no home of My own."

"I had an aunt and uncle who lived in Bethsaida." Dobah smiled at the memory of her last visit to Keziah. "I loved visiting there. The Sea of Galilee is beautiful. It calms my heart."

Yeshua looked at her. "You should return."

Dobah's heart seemed to leap in her chest. Return. To Galilee. To sit by the lake, to wade along its shore. She thought of the winter when she and Ethan visited Keziah. Rachel had been an infant sleeping in a basket. Levi had been a pudgy little three-year-old. Oh, how precious that time had been.

Lost in her memories, Dobah was scarcely aware they had reached the temple. Not until Yeshua stopped abruptly and spoke to a man standing before Him. "See, you are well again. Stop sinning, or something worse may happen to you."

Only then did Dobah recognize him as the lame man from the pool. He had neither a walking stick nor his pallet now. While he might need his pallet again when it was time to sleep, he no longer needed a cane.

The man nodded then turned and hurried away for the second time.

Yeshua healed him. I witnessed a miracle. I saw it happen. His leg changed before my eyes. The wonder of it washed over her for a second time. *We should return to Galilee. And not so I can sit by the lake.*

As Yeshua and His disciples moved deeper into the Court of the Gentiles, Dobah grasped Ethan's arm. "I want to follow Him."

Ethan gave her a questioning look.

"I want to learn from Him. Don't you?" Her grip on his arm tightened. "Ethan, we were there at the beginning. You followed the star. It brought you to my abba's house. You bowed before an infant because He was the promised King. The Messiah. Don't you want to be there for whatever comes next? How much longer could it be?"

"But the vineyard. Our responsibilities."

"Our sons know what to do. They can manage without us for a time."

Ethan's gaze shifted in the direction of Yeshua. "I suppose it would be possible."

Dobah grinned, more excited than she'd felt in years. Ethan smiled back at her then put a hand on her back and steered her through the crowd to catch up with Yeshua.

They'd just managed to do so when several Pharisees suddenly blocked Yeshua's path. One of them demanded to know if what he'd heard was true. Had Yeshua healed on Shabbat? Had He told the lame man to carry his pallet on Shabbat? Didn't Yeshua know the law?

Yeshua's expression was grave as He answered, "My Father is always at His work to this very day, and I too am working."

The Pharisees took a step back, as if standing so close to Yeshua was a dangerous thing.

"You dare to call Adonai Your Father? You dare to make Yourself equal with Him?"

"Very truly I tell you, the Son can do nothing by Himself; He can do only what He sees His Father doing, because whatever the

Father does the Son also does. For the Father loves the Son and shows Him all He does."

As Yeshua continued His reply to the Pharisees, Ethan leaned close to Dobah and softly said, "We will follow Him back to Galilee. We will see what His Father is doing because we will see what Yeshua is doing."

"We will follow Him now? When Pesach is over?"

"As soon as He and His *talmidim* start back, we will go too. You are right. Our sons can manage the vineyard without me for a season."

CHAPTER FORTY-ONE

Five days later, Ethan hitched a donkey to a cart. In the small wagon were a tent, blankets, and some changes of clothes, along with food and wine for the journey. Levi carried the last items from the house, dropped them into the cart, and then went to stand opposite Ethan, looking at him over the donkey's back.

"Are you certain about this, Abba?"

"We are certain."

"Imma is not the girl who went with you to Egypt. She is not used to camping under the stars. Perhaps you are asking too much of her."

Ethan chuckled. "Are you calling us old?"

"No," Levi answered—although both of them knew that was what he'd done.

Truth be told, Ethan sometimes felt old. He awakened in the mornings with aches and pains he didn't used to feel. However, nothing but death itself would have made him stay at home. He was as excited as his wife to be with Yeshua in Galilee. To sit with all those who followed Him and listen to His teaching. Ethan didn't expect to be a member of Yeshua's inner circle, but He could still be a disciple. He believed in Yeshua. He always had. But now that belief had moved from his head into his heart.

The memory of what Yeshua had said in the temple during Pesach played in his mind. *"Very truly I tell you, the Son can do nothing by Himself; He can do only what He sees His Father doing, because whatever the Father does the Son also does. For the Father loves the Son and shows Him all he does."*

A thrill ran through Ethan even now as he remembered. He believed. He believed in the One who had sent Yeshua. He believed the words Yeshua had spoken. Because of it, he could know he'd passed out of death into life. He wasn't sure how that happened or what it all meant, but he believed it was true.

He placed a hand on Levi's shoulder. "You know who He is, my son. You know why your imma and I must go."

Levi had heard the stories, of course. From an early age, Ethan and Dobah had told him of Yeshua's birth and the shepherds' declaration. He'd been told of the star that had led a khabir named Menes along with magi from the East to the humble home of Boaz ben David so they could worship the newborn King and lay gifts at the feet of His parents. Levi knew of Yosef's dream, of his parents' escape from Bethlehem, and of their flight into Egypt. But believing Yeshua—a man Levi thought of like a brother—was truly the promised Messiah? That was more difficult to digest.

"Perhaps it is you who should go to Galilee," Ethan said.

"No, Abba. I will stay and tend the vineyard with my brothers. You and Imma can tell us about it when you return. Just be careful."

"We will be. The roads are filled with pilgrims returning to their homes after Pesach. We will have company. And we are not far behind Yeshua and His followers. Perhaps we will even catch up with them if He stops to teach along the way. I have heard He often does that."

Dobah came out of the house, followed by their other sons and their wives and children. There was a great deal of hugging and even a few tears shed over their going.

When Dobah finally reached Ethan's side, he asked, "Do you want to ride, or walk for now?"

"I will walk beside you."

He leaned over and kissed her cheek. Then he took the donkey's lead, lifted a hand to wave to the family, and clucked his tongue to start the animal forward.

"They act as if we never mean to return," Dobah said, amusement in her voice.

"It may feel that way to them. You and I have not traveled farther away from Bethlehem than Jericho and Bethany for as far back as any of them can remember. Our relatives come from far away to be in Jerusalem during the festivals, but we are the ones always welcoming guests, not going to see others. When was the last time one of them wanted their imma or savta, and you have not been right there?"

"True."

They talked about everyday things as they walked, the cart creaking and rattling behind them. Bethlehem disappeared from view, and they were almost beyond the walls of Jerusalem when Dobah asked, "Do you ever regret the life we have had?"

The question so surprised Ethan that he stopped, and the donkey and Dobah did the same. "Why would you ask such a thing?"

A wisp of a smile curved her mouth. "If you had never come to Bethlehem, you might still be leading great caravans across the

Star of Wonder: Dobah's Story

length and width of the empire. You might be wealthy. You might be—"

"I might be many things, but none of them would matter without my faith in Adonai and my love for you and our children."

Her smile blossomed. How incredibly beautiful she was, even now with lines creasing the corners of her eyes and mouth, with gray sprinkled throughout her lovely hair.

"Come along." He tugged on the donkey's lead. "We want to get farther down the road before we make camp for the night."

"Levi thinks I am too old for this."

"Did he tell you that?"

"He did not have to."

"Well, you should know that he thinks I am too old for it too."

She laughed and reached to take hold of his hand as they walked on.

Thirty years had passed since Dobah had last made her bed beneath the stars on the road between Capernaum and Jerusalem. Thirty years. Despite all that had happened since that journey to stay with Keziah—the weddings that had been celebrated, the children and grandchildren who had been born, the deaths that had taken loved ones away—the number of years still managed to surprise her. And it was odd, how she could feel old and young at the same time.

"Are you comfortable?" Ethan asked, breaking the quiet of the night.

The fire he'd made earlier had burned low, but there was still enough light from it that she could see his face. "Has the earth grown harder over the years?"

He chuckled. "No."

"Produced a new crop of stones?"

"No."

"Then I must be as comfortable as I ever was."

"I was thinking again about the star that brought me to Bethlehem."

She rolled onto her side to face him. "You think about it often, don't you?"

"I suppose I do." He drew in a slow breath and released it. "I often wonder if anything like it will ever again appear in the heavens. Will Almighty God use it when it is time for Yeshua to be crowned? When Yeshua comes into His kingdom?"

"His kingdom," she echoed in a whisper.

Ethan rolled onto his side, mirroring her. "Is it about to happen, do you think? And how will it happen? I never expected to see opposition to the Messiah, but when I remember the anger of those Pharisees in the temple court on Shabbat, I wonder. Where is Yeshua's army? If the leaders of His own people are against Him, what then? How will He drive out the Romans?"

"That is why we are going to Galilee, Ethan. So we will know."

He raised up on an elbow, leaned forward, and kissed her forehead. "Yes." He lay back down. "Soon we will know. But I wish it had happened when I was a young man." He fell silent then, and it wasn't long before his slow and steady breathing told her he had fallen asleep.

But sleep continued to evade Dobah. Not because of the hard ground or the unexpected sounds in the night. No, it was memories of Yeshua that kept her awake. Through the years, she had doubted and believed, believed and doubted. But her lingering doubts had vanished by the pool of Bethesda when she'd seen Yeshua heal the man with a disability. Over the past year, they'd heard of Yeshua's other healings, including a leper, a paralyzed man, and a demoniac. Still, it was one thing to hear about a miracle. It was another to witness one with her own eyes.

She rolled onto her back and stared at the night sky.

How will it happen, Adonai? How will He be crowned? Where will it happen and when?

The stars overhead were not as bright as the one Ethan had followed all those years ago. Nowhere near as bright. But these stars on a moonless night reminded her of Adonai's majesty, of His power, of His creativity. Even of His goodness. They reminded her how very small she was and how mighty He was. She could study the Scriptures with her husband. They had done so throughout their marriage. But she would have answers to her questions only if the Lord of heaven's armies chose to reveal them to her.

I will trust and be alert to what You will show us.

She turned onto her side again, and at last, sleep overtook her.

CHAPTER FORTY-TWO

Dobah stared at the temporary shelters that dotted the land outside of Capernaum. "Why are there so many of them? What are they doing here?"

"They are here to see Yeshua," Ethan answered. "Just as we are."

He was right, of course. They'd talked to other people on the road over the past days. Many had been returning to Galilee after spending Pesach in Jerusalem. But others said they'd heard about the Rabbi, about His healing miracles, and they wanted to see Him for themselves.

"I still did not expect so many." She looked at her husband. "Is this dangerous?"

"For us?"

"For Yeshua."

Ethan's expression was grim. "It could be."

"Where do you suppose He is staying?"

"With one of His followers, probably."

She sighed. "We should have left Bethlehem sooner. We should have tried to catch up with Him before He reached Capernaum."

"We will find Him. Do not worry."

That old, fearful part of her nature tried to lift its head.

Adonai, You are my shepherd. She took a long, slow breath and released it. *I fear no evil, for You are with me.*

Ethan gave her a nod, as if he'd heard the silent words she used to push back her fear. Then he clucked to the donkey and gave a tug on the lead, moving them closer to the city of tents that had sprung up outside the gates of Capernaum.

Later, after they'd found a place to make camp, Ethan fed and watered the donkey while Dobah set out the last of the fruit and bread for them to eat.

When Ethan came to sit beside her, he said, "We will go into Capernaum. We can ask around about Yeshua and buy some food at the market." His gaze lifted toward other campsites. "If there is anything left for us to purchase."

Dobah hadn't considered that buying supplies could be a problem.

"And we will have to trust no one will steal the donkey while we are gone."

"I should stay here with our belongings."

"No. I would rather risk the donkey than you." He gave her a quick smile. "I will talk to the men staying over there." He motioned with his head. "I will ask them to keep an eye on our site."

"And if they are not honest?"

"Then Adonai will see to whatever happens next."

Dobah gave her head a quick shake. "No. Let's take the donkey and cart into Capernaum. We can sell them. We will keep with us only what we can carry."

"Dobah, what if Yeshua travels somewhere else?"

"Then we will walk the way others do. Or we will find another donkey to buy when the time comes. Others travel without an animal and cart. We can do the same."

"That is true." He cleared his throat. "I just hope we do not prove Levi right."

They finished eating their simple meal and then organized their belongings—what they would keep and what they thought they could do without—before Ethan hitched the donkey to the cart once more.

Located near the Via Maris—a major trade and military route connecting Egypt with Syria and Mesopotamia—Capernaum had a strong Roman presence whose mission was to protect the interests of the empire. As Dobah and Ethan approached the gates of the town, she saw many soldiers walking in pairs, looking for trouble of any kind.

Eyes averted, Dobah wondered, *Will these be the first Roman soldiers to be defeated by Yeshua?*

Not long after entering the town, Ethan found a buyer for both donkey and cart. In the marketplace, they were able to purchase some bread and more dried fruit.

"Do you know where we might find the rabbi, Yeshua?" Ethan asked one of the vendors.

The woman shook her head, but something in her expression told Dobah she might know more than she let on. "They must be asked that question a hundred times a day," she told Ethan as they walked away.

"You are right. They must." He smiled. "We will wait for Shabbat. We will find Him in the synagogue then."

Dobah supposed that was a logical plan, but she hated the idea of waiting. She was impatient to see Him again.

Early the next morning, Dobah and Ethan walked the short distance from their campsite to sit beside the Sea of Galilee and watch the sunrise as they ate their dried fruit. In companionable silence, they enjoyed the breeze off the water and the beauty of the lake with the light playing across its surface.

Lost in her thoughts, at first Dobah didn't notice the men walking along the shore. But as they drew closer, her eyes focused and recognition shot through her. "It is Him." She scrambled to her feet, and Ethan followed suit.

Yeshua stopped when He saw them. "Cousins! You came."

"As we said we would," Ethan answered.

"Where are you staying?"

Ethan motioned behind them at the small tent he'd erected the night before.

Yeshua moved closer. "You remember Simon. He and his wife have offered their kataluma for as long as you are with us."

"That is kind." Ethan nodded at the man standing near Yeshua. "We accept gratefully."

Simon, a tall man with a strong build, returned the nod.

"Come with us now," Yeshua said.

This was truly happening. Dobah and Ethan were now to be counted among the followers of the Messiah. Yeshua hadn't told them they were too old, and He hadn't excluded Dobah because she was a woman. He'd welcomed both of them and even arranged for a place to stay.

Dobah and Ethan, with the help of a few of Yeshua's followers, gathered their remaining belongings. As the group walked toward Capernaum, Dobah listened to the conversations of the men before and behind her. She sensed they were a tight community. Would she ever feel she fit in? As if reading her thoughts, Ethan reached for her hand and squeezed it.

Before they reached the gates of Capernaum, Yeshua was recognized. People began to approach them, pressing in. A woman pleaded for the healing of her son. A blind man begged for his sight. Yeshua slowed. He listened. He spoke. He touched.

Dobah stood on tiptoe, looking through the group of men who were closest to Yeshua. But as more and more people gathered, they closed ranks, and she could no longer see Him.

"Is it always like this?" Ethan asked someone nearby.

"These days, it is difficult for Yeshua to go anywhere and not have a crowd follow Him. He slips away in the mornings so He can be alone and pray, but the rest of the day, people are always looking for Him."

Dobah looked at the young man who had answered Ethan. She recognized him as someone who'd been with Yeshua in Jerusalem. He'd been close by at the pool of Bethesda.

"I am Philip," he added.

Ethan answered, "Ethan and Dobah."

"I know." He met Dobah's eyes. "You are the cousin of Yosef, Miryam's husband."

"Yes, I am."

"Yeshua has spoken of you both." Philip pointed. "I can take you to Simon's house if you like. If we go that way, we can get around this crowd. Yeshua will likely be here for a while."

Dobah tried to see through the crowd again, but Yeshua remained hidden from her view. More voices called out to Him, cries of delight mingled with them. People were being healed, and she longed to see it for herself.

Ethan said, "We should go with Philip."

She wanted to refuse. Wouldn't it be better to find higher ground instead?

"We will find Him again later." Ethan took her arm and eased her after Philip who had already started walking away.

Like fish swimming upstream, they made their way toward Capernaum as more and more people flowed away from the encampments near the town gates, the news of Yeshua's whereabouts spreading. They were near the market area where Dobah and Ethan had purchased food the previous day when six Roman soldiers marched by, headed toward the gates.

"They watch Yeshua," Philip said. "Both the Romans and the Pharisees watch Him."

Ethan took a step closer to Dobah. "That cannot make life easy."

Philip shook his head. "I do not believe following Him is meant to be easy."

From long ago came the memory of the temple and an old man named Simeon on the day of Yeshua's dedication. *"The child is destined to cause the falling and rising of many in Israel, and to be a sign that will be spoken against, so that the thoughts of many hearts will be revealed. And a sword will pierce your own soul too."*

"Following Him is not meant to be easy," she whispered, feeling the truth of those words take hold of her heart.

CHAPTER FORTY-THREE

Dobah was relieved to discover she was not the only woman among Yeshua's followers. There were a number of women who had been healed by Him, including one called Magdalene who had been set free of seven demons.

Yeshua did not give Dobah and Ethan special attention as members of His own family. Yet Dobah didn't feel less than anyone else. She wasn't sure how He did it, with so many vying for attention, but He always made people feel loved and seen.

A few weeks after Dobah and Ethan's arrival in Capernaum, Yeshua slipped away for a night of solitary prayer on the mountain. When He returned the next day, He called together His disciples. There were about seventy men among His followers, and from them, He called out twelve and named them apostles, men chosen to be His emissaries. By this time, Dobah knew each one of the twelve, at least a little. They were different in age, size, and temperament, but they were the same in their devotion to their Rabbi, fervent in their belief in Yeshua as the Messiah.

Observing the moment with her husband, Dobah felt a stirring within. An excitement for what was to come. But some trepidation as well. A great throng of people surrounded Yeshua that day, as on other days, eager to hear Him speak, anxious for Him to heal their diseases and cast out unclean spirits. They'd come from Judea and Jerusalem, from Tyre and Sidon, from the Decapolis and from beyond the Jordan. They pressed in, wanting to touch Him, seeking the power that came out of Him.

"He is more than a warrior king," Dobah said to Ethan. "Isn't He?"

"Yes. He is more than a man too."

For these past weeks in Capernaum, Dobah had sat at Yeshua's feet, listening and learning. She treasured the stories He told to His followers, to all who would listen. Sometimes she understood a lesson at once. Other times she had to wrestle to make sense of the meaning. Some things she had yet to understand, no matter how hard she tried.

On this day, Yeshua moved through the throng, climbing up the side of a mountain, the people following. Ethan took Dobah's arm, and they did the same. When Yeshua stopped at last, looking as if He'd found the place that pleased Him, He faced the crowd and motioned for them to sit. Ethan drew Dobah onto a nearby hillside for a better view. A hush began to fall over the people. The anticipation was palpable.

"Blessed are the poor in spirit, for theirs is the kingdom of heaven," Yeshua began at last, His voice carrying down the mountainside. "Blessed are those who mourn, for they will be comforted. Blessed are the meek, for they will inherit the earth. Blessed are those who hunger and thirst for righteousness, for they will be filled."

Dobah's breath was shallow. She didn't want to risk missing a single word.

"Blessed are the merciful, for they will be shown mercy. Blessed are the pure in heart, for they will see God."

Dobah sat mesmerized, along with the multitude.

Yeshua was, indeed, more than a mere man.

Ethan wasn't aware of the passage of time. Like his wife and others around them, he listened to Yeshua and tried to absorb all that He said.

That prayer. *Our Father in heaven.* He wanted to remember that prayer. He wanted to pray it always.

But seek first His kingdom and His righteousness, and all these things will be given to you as well. He must remember that too. Remember what is eternally important. Adonai must come first in his life. Then everything else would fall into place.

"If you, then, though you are evil, know how to give good gifts to your children, how much more will your Father in heaven give good gifts to those who ask Him!" Asking for what is good from his Father in heaven. He'd never thought of prayer in quite that way.

Despite how long Yeshua had been speaking by that time, His voice rose as He said, "Therefore everyone who hears these words of Mine and puts them into practice is like a wise man who built his house on the rock. The rain came down, the streams rose, and the winds blew and beat against that house; yet it did not fall, because it had its foundation on the rock."

Yeshua stopped speaking, and the silence itself seemed loud. Even the birds were quiet. Only when it became obvious that His teaching was over did people begin to talk among themselves.

"He is not like the scribes," someone nearby said. "He teaches with real authority."

"You have no idea," Ethan whispered to himself, his gaze roaming over the crowd.

He noticed a small group of Pharisees close to the foot of the mountainside. He also noticed Roman soldiers scattered throughout the crowd. Had they listened? Had they understood? Any of them? Jew or gentile? He looked at Dobah, prepared to ask what she thought.

"Ethan?" a deep voice interrupted.

He turned his head farther and saw a man standing with the sun now behind him. Ethan shaded his eyes then rose to his feet, still uncertain who had spoken his name.

"It *is* you."

Surprise shot through him as recognition came. "Atticus?"

It was close to twenty-nine years since he'd last seen Atticus Barba. That time, too, it had been near the Sea of Galilee. But unlike before, Atticus didn't wear the uniform of a Roman soldier. Instead he was clothed in the tunic and robe of a well-to-do citizen.

"I cannot believe it," Atticus said, gripping Ethan by the upper arms and grinning broadly. "After all these years."

A sense of confusion remained. "Have you been in Capernaum all this time?"

"No." Atticus chuckled as he released his grip on Ethan. "I finished my twenty-five years of service in another corner of the empire. But after I received my Roman citizenship, I returned to Galilee. Like my father before me, I now import and export goods. Wine, spices, textiles. Capernaum is in a convenient location along the trade route. It has served my business well."

Movement on Ethan's right pulled his gaze to Dobah. He gently drew her to his side. "Atticus, this is my wife, Dobah."

Atticus's smile softened, and he offered a bow. "It is my pleasure to meet you at last, good lady."

Ethan wondered if Dobah remembered Atticus from all those years ago. They'd never met, but she'd seen him the day after the big storm, the Roman soldier on the streets of Bethsaida.

"You are Ethan's friend," she said, answering his unspoken question. "From the caravan when he was a boy."

Atticus's eyes shifted to Ethan. "I am his friend still, I hope."

"And you came to hear Yeshua teach?" she asked.

"This is not the first time I have listened to Him. The Rabbi's words...intrigue me." He looked around the hillside, watching the crowd as it slowly began to disperse. "But they anger others."

"We know," Ethan said. "We follow Him."

Surprise flashed across Atticus's face as he returned his gaze to Ethan. "Then you should be careful, my friend. And warn Him. Rome does not approve of Him or His followers. They fear insurrection."

"But did you hear Yeshua say anything about insurrection?" Ethan shook his head. "No. He said to make friends with those who oppose us. He said to turn the other cheek. He said to love our enemies and to pray for them."

Atticus shook his head slowly. "It is not His words that upset those in charge. It is all the people flowing into Galilee to listen to Him. Romans like order. This"—he motioned with a hand toward the people who remained on the hillside—"is not orderly. And your own leaders resent His popularity among the people. I fear there is trouble ahead for Him."

That night, in the guest room of Simon's house, Dobah reached for her husband's hand in the darkness, knowing he was awake, like her. "Will you see your friend again?" she asked.

"Atticus? Yes. I would like to. As long as we remain in Capernaum."

"He did not seem surprised when you called Yeshua the Messiah."

"No, he did not."

"But does he believe in Yeshua as we do?"

"I do not know, Dobah. I would guess not yet. But something has drawn him to listen to Yeshua's teachings. If he keeps listening, perhaps he will know and believe."

"Like you," she whispered.

"Like me."

"Remember when you said nothing was impossible for Adonai? Not even bringing Atticus to believe."

"I remember."

"And today your Roman friend was present, listening to the Messiah give a great message."

Ethan chuckled softly. "He was there. He was listening."

"You have believed in Him from the moment the star led you to Bethlehem."

"I have." He squeezed her hand. "Remember what Philip said to us when we first came to Capernaum. That following Yeshua wasn't meant to be easy. I think he is right. And I think it is going to get harder. After listening to Him speak today, Dobah, I don't believe He will be the sort of king many have expected. The kind even I expected."

She pictured Yeshua on the hillside earlier in the day, and Simeon's words returned to her once more. *"And a sword will pierce your own soul too."* Tears sprang to her eyes. "Were we wrong to come to Galilee?" she whispered, her throat tight with emotion.

"No, Dobah. We were not wrong. We will follow Him the same way I followed the star. We will follow where He leads. Wherever He takes us."

EPILOGUE

Two years later, in the month of Sivan, 30 AD

Dobah looked at her grandchildren, seated on the floor at the foot of her stool. "For more than a year, your saba and I followed Yeshua all around Galilee. We even followed Him to the Decapolis. We saw Him heal lepers and blind men and those who couldn't walk. We saw Him feed five thousand men, plus the women and children, from five loaves and two fish."

Even the oldest of her grandchildren listened closely, although they'd heard the stories many times before. Her children and their spouses, seated with backs against the wall, also listened. Some wore smiles. Others revealed skepticism, although not hostility.

Ethan took her hand and said, "We saw Yeshua perform many miracles. But the miracles had a purpose. They weren't for the sake of miracles alone. They weren't to help raise an army. They were meant to show His people who He really is. The Messiah who is bringing the kingdom of God to Earth."

Dobah smiled. Her husband wasn't a rabbi, but he was able to teach others and often did so in homes in Jerusalem.

"After our time with Yeshua in Galilee," he continued, "He brought His followers to Judea, and your savta and I were able to come home. We were able to see all of you again. And that made our hearts happy. But we were with Yeshua often in Jerusalem and Bethany. We continued to learn from Him. We continued to discover all the Tanakh has to say about Him."

Tears welled in Dobah's eyes. "Still, we did not fully understand He would have to suffer for us. That He would do so willingly. And when He died on that cross, we did not truly believe He would rise on the third day, even though He told us He would."

"Savta," five-year-old Hannah asked, "can we go see Yeshua?"

Dobah leaned forward and cupped the girl's face. "No, Hannah. Yeshua ascended to heaven and is seated at the right hand of the Father. Some of His followers saw Him taken up with their own eyes. But you and I will see Him again when He returns from heaven, the same way He left. We do not know when that will be, but we will keep looking up in anticipation."

Ethan said, "The church in Jerusalem is growing every day. His disciples teach daily in the temple. The gift of the Ruach HaKodesh has been given to all those who believe, to all who have turned from sin, returned to God, and been baptized in the authority of His name. Day after day, Adonai keeps adding to those who are saved. We pray each one of you will be among them."

Dobah blinked away another wave of tears. Some of their children believed Yeshua was the Messiah. So did most of their grandchildren. But not all, and her heart ached for those who could not yet understand.

A year ago, Levi and his wife Aziel had heard Yeshua teach in the temple and been persuaded to believe in Him. As for Rachel and her husband, Dan, they lived in Bethany, and when their neighbor Lazarus was raised from the dead, they had come to believe as well, along with Dan's parents and brothers and sisters. Noah and his wife also believed.

Dobah would go on sharing her stories with all her family. She would go on praying for each one of them too. She would trust in God's faithfulness. After all, if Adonai could bring a khabir from the east, a bright star leading the way, if He could use that khabir to rescue a widow and her son and prolong their lives, if that man could become a ger tzedek and be given a new name, if he and the woman could marry and be given many children and grandchildren, then Adonai could also draw all of her family to believe in Messiah Yeshua.

She recalled the words of Simon, now called Peter, on the day of Pentecost, and her heart was stirred again. *"The promise is for you and your children and for all who are far off—for all whom the Lord our God will call."*

Once Dobah had been a woman of many doubts. Once she had let fear dwell in her heart. But the resurrection of her Lord had put an end to those things for good. There was no shadow of doubt left in her faith nor would she allow fear to overcome her. As Ethan had said to her one night in Capernaum, she would follow Yeshua the same way Ethan had followed that star. Wherever He took them, they would go.

The way was bright before them.

FROM THE AUTHOR

Dear Reader,

I love writing biblical fiction because I get to spend a great deal of time in the Word as well as researching the culture and customs and the land itself where Christianity was birthed. I hope you feel the same when you read my story.

Over the past fifteen years, I have learned so much about reading my Bible through a Middle Eastern lens, learning to understand the Word by understanding the people it was first written for. Every age and every culture has its own idioms. If I say, "You can't teach an old dog..." you automatically answer, "New tricks." That's an American idiom. There are Jewish idioms included in the Bible that we miss if we aren't reading through the right lens.

It really helped me to understand the Christmas story when I learned from Bible scholars that kataluma, translated "inn" in Luke 2:7 in many translations, is correctly translated as "guest room." (It is unlikely Luke meant a commercial inn, because when he wrote about the Good Samaritan in Luke 10:34, he used *pandocheion*, which was a commercial inn.) With Bethlehem filled to overflowing because of the census, most people's guest rooms were already occupied by friends, relatives, and even strangers. Most modest homes had a stable built into them. The animals were separated from the living quarters by very little. It was not unthinkable for a woman to give birth in a stable (after it had been properly cleaned) because it would have allowed both a place to stay and also a bit of privacy. In a hospitality culture, someone would have made certain Mary and Joseph had a roof over their heads for the birth of Jesus.

The Star of Bethlehem was the initial inspiration for this story, but its appearance is brief in Scripture. The idea for my hero to be the khabir who brought the wise men to Bethlehem came to me quickly, and then I knew my heroine had to be a widow with a son under the age of two because of what happened when the wise men didn't return to Herod. And what if that widow was somehow related to Joseph? I loved the idea of a relative being in Bethlehem at the time of Jesus's birth, someone who would see Him as a baby who had to be fed and changed, someone who could watch Him grow into a boy and then a man. Wouldn't that make it hard to believe Him divine? Even the Lord's own brother James didn't believe in Him until after the resurrection.

It was a true adventure for me to take Dobah and Menes/Ethan to Alexandria. I had so much to learn. That city is only one possible location where Joseph and Mary might have lived during their exile, but it was the largest city in the known world with a very large Jewish population, so I chose to take them there. Also, the length of their stay in Egypt is undetermined. However, we know they didn't return until Herod's death, and we do know when that happened.

Warm regards,
Robin Lee Hatcher

THE STAR OF BETHLEHEM

By Reverend Jane Willan MS, MDiv

The Star of Bethlehem is one of history's most intriguing intersections of faith, mystery, and science. It is said to have guided the magi, or wise men, to the birthplace of Jesus. The star's appearance marks a pivotal moment in Christianity, a symbol of divine guidance and the fulfillment of ancient prophecies.

Throughout the Bible, stars are crucial in conveying God's messages and marking moments of cosmic importance. In Psalm 147:4, we read, "He determines the number of the stars and calls them each by name." This verse demonstrates a personal connection between the holy and the stars. This idea of stars as divinely appointed guides would have resonated with the magi who followed the Star of Bethlehem.

Stars also frequently appear in biblical prophecies. In Genesis 15:5, God makes a covenant with Abraham, saying, "Look up at the sky and count the stars—if indeed you can count them... So shall your offspring be." This promise of innumerable descendants is later echoed in various passages, linking the stars to God's faithfulness and the destiny of His chosen people.

The prophet Daniel, known for his apocalyptic visions, also uses celestial imagery. In Daniel 12:3, he writes, "Those who are wise will shine like the brightness of the heavens, and those who lead many to righteousness, like the stars forever and ever." Here, stars represent not only divine favor but also the eternal nature of righteousness.

The appearance of the Star of Bethlehem would have been interpreted as a clear sign of God's activity. Its unique behavior—guiding the magi to a specific location—sets it apart as a special messenger, announcing the birth of a king whose coming had been foretold by the prophets.

The account of the Star of Bethlehem is found in the Gospel of Matthew, chapter 2. The narrative begins with the arrival of the magi in Jerusalem, asking, "Where is the one who has been born king of the Jews? We saw his star when it rose and have come to worship him" (Matthew 2:2).

This passage is remarkable for several reasons. First, it introduces the magi, who are described as coming "from the East." These figures were likely astronomers or scholars from Persia or Babylon, regions known for their advanced understanding of astronomy. Their journey to Jerusalem based on the appearance of a star speaks to the widespread belief in celestial signs as indicators of earthly events.

After leading the magi to Jerusalem, the star reappears and shows them the direction to Bethlehem: "After they had heard the king, they went on their way, and the star they had seen when it rose went ahead of them until it stopped over the place where the child was" (Matthew 2:9).

This description suggests that the Star of Bethlehem was no ordinary celestial body. Its ability to move and then stop over a specific location sets it apart from typical stellar behavior. This unusual characteristic has led to centuries of debate about the nature of the star and what it might have been.

The reaction of the magi to the star's guidance is equally significant: "When they saw the star, they were overjoyed" (Matthew 2:10). Their response underscores the star's role as both a navigational aid and a source of spiritual confirmation and joy. For the magi, the star was a divine sign, leading them to the completion of their quest.

To fully appreciate the impact of the Star of Bethlehem on those who witnessed it, we need to understand the astronomical knowledge and beliefs of people in the first century. In the ancient world, celestial observations were often intertwined with religious and prophetic interpretations. The magi would have been well-versed in the mathematical calculations of celestial movements and interpreting these movements as signs.

The prevailing model of the universe in the first century was the geocentric model, which placed the Earth at the center of creation. The stars were believed to be fixed points of light on a celestial sphere that rotated around the Earth. Planets, known as "wandering stars," moved in complex patterns against that backdrop.

This understanding of the cosmos as a series of ever-larger spheres with the Earth at the center was not just a scientific model but also a philosophical and religious one. It reinforced the idea of humanity's central place in creation and the belief that events in the heavens directly corresponded to events on Earth.

Despite the limitations of their model, ancient astronomers were remarkably adept at observing and predicting celestial events. They carefully tracked the movements of planets, noted the appearance of comets, and recorded unusual phenomena like eclipses and supernovas.

Over the centuries, scholars, astronomers, and theologians have proposed various theories to explain the nature of the Star of Bethlehem. One popular theory suggests that it may have been a rare alignment of planets known as a conjunction. Proponents of this theory often point to a triple conjunction of Jupiter and Saturn that occurred in 7 BC in the constellation Pisces.

Jupiter was often associated with kingship in ancient traditions, while Saturn was sometimes linked to the Jewish people. The constellation Pisces was sometimes associated with Israel. Therefore, this rare alignment could have been interpreted as a sign of a new king of the Jews.

Although this theory aligns with a known astronomical event that would have been noticeable to ancient observers, it doesn't easily explain the star's described movement. However, another theory proposes that the Star of Bethlehem may have been a comet. Chinese astronomical records note the appearance of a comet in 5 BC, which some researchers have linked to the Star of Bethlehem.

Comets, with their distinctive appearance and movement across the sky, could account for the star's described behavior in Matthew's gospel. Similarly, a supernova—the explosive death of a star—could have appeared as a bright new star in the heavens.

Despite centuries of study, the exact nature of the Star of Bethlehem remains a mystery. Each theory has its strengths and weaknesses, and the lack of conclusive evidence allows for ongoing debate and exploration without definitive answer. But this mystery only adds to our enduring fascination and the star's symbolic power.

For all of us, regardless of belief or background, the Star of Bethlehem offers a moment to pause and contemplate. In a world often focused on the immediate and explainable, it invites us to consider the possibility and wonder of the extraordinary breaking into the ordinary.

So, as we gaze up at the night sky, we should remember the magi of old, following a star to an unexpected destination. Their journey reminds us that sometimes the most profound truths are found not in the grandeur of palaces but in the humility of a stable—and that wisdom often comes from being willing to follow the light, wherever it may lead.

Fiction Author

ROBIN LEE HATCHER

Robin Lee Hatcher is the author of over ninety novels and novellas with over five million copies in print. Her well-drawn characters and heartwarming stories of faith, courage, and love have earned her both critical acclaim and the devotion of readers. Her numerous awards include the Christy Award for Excellence in Christian Fiction, the RITA® Award for Best Inspirational Romance, Romantic Times Career Achievement Awards for Americana Romance and for Inspirational Fiction, the Carol Award, the 2011 Idahope Writer of the Year, and Lifetime Achievement Awards from both Romance Writers of America® (2001) and American Christian Fiction Writers (2014).

Robin began her writing career in the general market, writing mass-market romances. In 1997, Robin felt called to write stories of faith and hasn't looked back since. She writes both contemporary and historical women's fiction and romance.

When not writing, Robin enjoys being with her family, spending time in the beautiful Idaho outdoors, Bible art journaling, reading books that make her cry, watching romantic movies, and decorative planning. She makes her home on the outskirts of Boise, sharing it with a demanding papillon dog and a persnickety tuxedo cat.

Nonfiction Author

REVEREND JANE WILLAN, MS, MDiv

Reverend Jane Willan writes contemporary women's fiction, mystery novels, church newsletters, and a weekly sermon.

Jane loves to set her novels amid church life. She believes that ecclesiology, liturgy, and church lady drama make for twisty plots and quirky characters. When not working at the church or creating new adventures for her characters, Jane relaxes at her favorite local bookstore, enjoying coffee and a variety of carbohydrates with frosting. Otherwise, you might catch her binge-watching a streaming series or hiking through the Connecticut woods with her husband and rescue dog, Ollie.

Jane earned a Bachelor of Arts degree from Hiram College, majoring in Religion and History, a Master of Science degree from Boston University, and a Master of Divinity from Vanderbilt University.

Read on for a sneak peek of another exciting story in the Mysteries & Wonders of the Bible series!

SWEET GIFT FROM HEAVEN:
Rana's Story

BY ANNE DAVIDSON

It would take more than the waters of the mighty Nile turning into blood to frighten Rana. It would take more than locusts, or hail and fire raining down from the sky, or even three days of total darkness. Fear? That did not come from the plagues the Hebrew slaves believed were sent by their God. Fear came from hunger and from want. Fear rose in her on those nights when the stars glittered like knives above her as she slept on the ground and her feet were cold and she found herself wondering if, at some time she could no longer remember that she ever had a home and a family.

Even that morning when the people at the marketplace cried and wailed and talked about what had happened the night before, when the God of the Hebrews prowled the land of Egypt like a hungry lion and killed its firstborn, she was not afraid. She was alive. She was a survivor. Her strength and her cleverness, those were what kept the fear at bay.

When she was yet a child, she learned to be quick and quiet so that she might pilfer bread from the sellers at the market or snatch up a trinket or two from the homes of the wealthy. Since she had come into her womanhood, she had discovered how her smile could dazzle men in the taverns so that they forgot the grilled wild fowl they ate, and the beer they drank, and the fact that their purses were within easy reach of her nimble fingers.

A survivor, yes, as she would be that day, and always.

Telling herself not to forget it, she waited while a small, bent man at the market stall in Pharaoh's treasure city of Pithom fell into conversation with an old woman whose cheeks were stained with tears.

"My son, my son!" The old woman's hands were like claws, and she twisted them together and wept. "Taken from me in the dark. And his oldest gone too. I am a widow, and my son and my grandson cared for me. What will I do now?"

"You will do all you have to," Rana whispered, not because the woman could hear her but to remind herself. "Just as I do." The man put his hand on the woman's shoulder to console her, and they cried together, and Rana saw her opportunity. There was a basket nearby piled with amulets made in the shape of lizards. Pretty, shiny things. The treasure city of Pithom was dedicated to Atum, god of the evening sun, and the lizard was sacred to him. If she could scoop up five or more of the baubles and sell them to Zoser, the one-eyed man always eager to accept what she brought him and ask no questions, she could eat bread and drink beer for three days. She would not need to live with the hunger.

Her gaze fixed on the man and the old woman, she snaked a hand to the basket. It was early. The metal charms were cool to the touch, and she snatched up a handful of them. She was just about to tuck them under her linen sheath when she heard voices raised behind her.

"Stop! Thief!"

Rana's heart slammed against her ribs, yet she stood as still as the statue of the Pharaoh—all life and praise to him!—that looked over the nearby complex of buildings where grain was stored. She dared not look guilty, or she would surely attract attention. But she could not seem unconcerned, either, for that in itself would make her look suspicious. Like the other people in the marketplace, she glanced around to see what the commotion was about.

Now her heart beat in double time, so forcefully, she thought it would burst from her chest. Three of the Medjay, Pharaoh's dreaded police, marched toward her, the muscles of their arms and legs bulging in the morning sunlight, their wooden staffs raised, their gazes fixed on her.

And in that moment when her breath caught and her blood ran cold, she knew that though the God of the Hebrews did not frighten her, the thought of being captured for her crime did. She did not wish to have her fingers cut off or her nose sliced from her face as punishment.

Rana took off running. Still, she was no fool. She kept a tight grip on the lizard amulets while she darted around the market stall, rushed past a man selling figs, and sprinted toward the grain storehouse built with bricks made by the Hebrew slaves from mud and straw. There, she stopped in the shadows but only long enough to catch her breath. The Medjay were not far away. She could hear them call to one another, and she was glad they did not have one of their dogs or monkeys with them. Being stopped by the lash of a Medjay rod would be bad enough. Being ripped apart by the teeth of one of their hounds or the claws of a vicious monkey would be even worse.

A second of rest, no more, and she started running again. She did not look over her shoulder. She didn't have to. She heard the footfalls of the Medjay behind her and, breathless, she whispered a prayer to the great god, Set, who had once stolen the body of Osiris from the embalmer. Being a thief too, Set would surely understand. Set would rescue her.

When she rounded a corner, she saw the answer to her prayer. A donkey cart blocked her path. Rana was young and limber, so she ducked under the cart, scrambled across the dusty ground, and leaped to her feet on the other side. The Medjay were large men, and even as she heard them yell for the driver to move along, she smiled and thanked Set for his kindness.

She knew she did not have the luxury of basking in her small victory. Here on the far side of the storage buildings were the homes of the craftsmen of Pithom, the painters who decorated Pharaoh's temples. The stonemasons who carved his statues. The dwellings here were small and simple, and from some of them, she heard the wailing of mourners. But one, very close by, was silent, and if it was empty, it would be the perfect place to hide.

No sooner was Rana through the doorway, though, than she froze. This worker was a firstborn son, surely. He lay on his low-slung bed, his cheeks sunken, his vacant eyes staring at the ceiling and at the flies that buzzed around his face.

"I am sorry to disturb you," she told him, knowing at the same time she could not afford to ignore the opportunity his silence presented. A quick look over her shoulder, and she slipped under the bed.

With her stomach pressed to the earthen floor, she had a unique perspective of the home's doorway. She saw the Medjay rumble past and breathed a sigh of relief. Until she heard one man call to the others to come back.

Three pairs of feet stopped in the doorway. Three rods held at the sides of six muscular legs.

"You think she has come in here?" one of the men asked. "There is death in this house. She would not dare."

"A thief will dare anything if she is desperate enough." The voice of this man was thick and raspy. He stepped into the dwelling and paused, and though Rana could see no more than his reed sandals and muscled shins, she knew he was taking a close look around. "A firstborn son," he said. He was surely looking right at the body, right at the bed.

"They say the Hebrew God is powerful," another of the men replied. "Even Pharaoh trembles before him. He has ordered the Hebrews to leave this land."

"Has he?" The man with the raspy voice spat on the ground. "I had not heard. It seems Pharoah has surrendered too easily."

"With plague upon the land—"

The man with the raspy voice barked a curse. "Pharaoh is a god, is he not? He can exact his own revenge."

"Yes," one of the other men replied. "But now that Pharaoh's own son is dead—"

"Firstborn."

Raspy Voice snapped, "I would see to it that the Hebrews were slaughtered for their insolence."

"They have strong magic," the first man reminded him.

"But our little thief does not. And I tell you this, friends, if I ever see her again, my rod will be the least of her worries." Rana did not need to see his face. She knew it was twisted with anger. Wherever she was, he wanted her to hear. He thundered his words. "I will kill you with my own bare hands, little thief. I will feed your body to the crocodiles in the mighty Nile."

"Then we had best be off and find her." The other two men moved again to the doorway. "Come along, Asim. The sooner we find this thief, the sooner you can use your rod to teach her a lesson."

Asim whipped his wooden rod through the air, and it whooshed and buzzed as Rana squeezed her eyes shut and cringed.

When he and the other Medjay walked out of the dwelling, she released the breath she'd been holding.

She didn't move, not for a very long time, and when she finally pulled herself out from under the bed and went again to the door, she peeked out the doorway, left and right.

There was no sign of the Medjay. "Thank you, great Set," she whispered, as she slipped from the house.

Outside, a woman balancing a basket on her head eyed Rana carefully. A man leading a calf on a tether looked her over. A child, his eyes shining with excitement, pointed a finger. "This is the one," he called out. "The one the Medjay are searching for."

She did not wait to hear more. Had the Medjay gone farther into the district of the craftsmen? Rana ran back toward the marketplace, the way she'd come.

She did not have a plan, at least not at first. It was not until she realized that her hand was still gripping the lizard amulets that she knew she might yet find a way to save herself.

With the thief and Medjay gone, the marketplace had settled again into its routine. Women picked at the figs and dates. Men gathered in tight circles, some of them weeping. Others were off to the side, grinding grain. Rana kept herself to the perimeter of the market, her gaze focused ahead of her on the grand temple of Atum. It was a glorious building, and looking at the statues outside it—the pharaohs and gods, huge and majestic—never failed to fill her with awe. But it was not wonderment she was after. Instead, she searched the shadows at the far side of the temple. There, outside one of the outbuildings used by the men who maintained the temple and its environs, she found what she was looking for.

Zoser was a man of substance, the thief all others looked up to, the one who told them where to find the pilgrims with their heavy purses, or the soldiers, drunk on beer and too careless with their gold. He was the one who accepted the items they brought to him. In exchange, he gave them bread and, if the items they presented were especially valuable, he might even offer a place for them to sleep in the courtyard of his home.

Zoser was propped against the building, dozing, his chin on the bulge of his stomach, and Rana wasted no time. She closed in on him and stuck out her hand, revealing the lizard amulets. "I have these."

Her voice startled him. His head came up. His right eye had been taken by the Medjay in the days when Zoser himself prowled the streets as Rana did now, and he had to swivel his head and squint with this good eye to see what she held out to him. He sniffed. His fat fingers wrapped around Rana's wrist and yanked her hand closer to his good eye. "Worthless," he mumbled.

Rana refused to lose heart. She swallowed hard. "One or two, perhaps, would not be worth your interest. But if I give you all five…"

His eye sparked with sudden interest. "Give?"

She nodded. "All five."

"For what in return?"

"No bread. No beer. Just…" His fingers tightened around her wrist, but Rana dared not pull her hand away. Zoser had always reminded her of a jackal god, keen and ruthless, yet she refused to let him know that the touch of his hand made her insides writhe like a snake. "I want only to take shelter in your dwelling."

When he laughed, Zoser's stomach quivered. "The Medjay are looking for you?"

She nodded.

"What have you done?"

"Just"—she moved her hand as much as she was able—"these."

"Small things. And hardly enough."

"But…" She hated that her voice quavered.

"But…" Zoser put up a hand. "Ten days of thieving. That is my price. You give me these small things, and you spend ten days giving me all you gather. And you ask nothing in return."

It was an outrageous bargain, but Rana knew she had no choice. She tamped down her anger and swallowed the epithets on her tongue. "Yes," she whispered, and when Zoser tilted his head as if he hadn't heard, she raised her voice and spoke again. "Yes, I will do it. But in return, you must—"

"Yes, yes. I know." His hand still tight around her wrist, Zoser hauled himself to his feet with a grunt. He was not a tall man, and when he stood before her, his stout belly nearly touched hers. He gave her a close look, slipped his tongue over his lips, and called out, "I have her! Come collect the thief!"

The three Medjay emerged from the nearby workroom.

Rana's mouth fell open. The breath caught in her throat. "You cannot!" She struggled to free herself from Zoser, but his grip was tight. He grinned. The Medjay, their rods raised, closed in. And Rana knew she had only one hope. She bit the hand that held her, as hard as she could.

Zoser howled like a hyena, and when he jumped back, he loosened his hold on her. Rana did not waste a moment. Before the Medjay could get nearer, she whirled and ran.

Past the workers' houses. Through an alleyway. She shot out from between two buildings and found herself in a district she was not familiar with, where the dwellings were smaller even than the craftsmen's homes. It was a silent, forlorn place that looked abandoned. No sounds of voices or of the weeping she'd heard earlier. No animals. No people. She leaped over an empty basket in the middle of the pathway and skirted a pile of broken crockery. She ran until she came to an enclosure, and when she jumped the barrier, she startled a shepherd working at the far end of it to gather his sheep and goats. The man was clothed in wool.

She knew then that she was in the heart of Goshen, where the Hebrew slaves lived, for the Israelite people spun and wove the wool of their animals, while Egyptians made their cloth from linen.

Try as she might, Rana could not remember if she'd ever heard enough about the Hebrews to know if they welcomed or feared the Medjay. If she was discovered, would the slaves hand her over with as much glee as Zoser had?

She couldn't take the chance of finding out.

She darted through the flock and past the shepherd, and because of the quiet, she heard a grunt and curses when one of the Medjay tripped and fell somewhere behind her. The others did not stop, their footfalls echoing through the silence.

Another alleyway, and though Rana was tempted to stop there, to press herself against the wall and hope she was not discovered, she did not. The pathway between the buildings twisted right and left, and she followed it, emerging into a large square engulfed in complete chaos. It was no wonder she had not encountered another soul except the shepherd. It seemed as if all of Goshen was gathered here.

Women and children stacked baskets and textiles into carts to which men hitched mules. Old women hurried by, urns of water on their heads. Children dragged each other by the hand, encouraged by the shouts of their mothers. And all around her, voices were raised in what sounded to Rana like a song of praise, a song of new beginnings and freedom.

Not for her. Not if she was discovered.

Rana looked over her shoulder just in time to see the two remaining Medjay emerge from the alley. She had little time. And few options.

There was a cart up ahead loaded with wool waiting to be spun, and as the man who should be attending it was busy helping an old woman onto the seat at the front of the cart, Rana slipped into the back. She scooted as far from the back of the cart as she was able until she was pressed to the far end of it, grabbing handfuls of wool as she did and piling them in front of her, a wall to shelter and hide her.

"Where is she?" Asim, the Medjay, called out, but no one answered him. They were too busy securing their possessions to the backs of mules, gathering their families, praising their God. "Has anyone seen the thief?" he shouted. "For if you have, you will be rewarded with Pharaoh's gratitude."

In all the turbulence, Rana was surprised to catch a glimmer of laughter from the driver of the cart. "We are free men, setting off on the road and meeting up with Moses and the others who are coming from Rameses. Your pharaoh is our master no longer."

With that, the cart lurched forward. Wherever it was going, Rana knew it didn't matter. She would slip from the cart in the darkness and make her way back to Pithom. For now, though, she was safe.

She too was on the road to freedom.

A NOTE FROM THE EDITORS

We hope you enjoyed another exciting volume in the Mysteries & Wonders of the Bible series, published by Guideposts. For over seventy-five years, Guideposts, a nonprofit organization, has been driven by a vision of a world filled with hope. We aspire to be the voice of a trusted friend, a friend who makes you feel more hopeful and connected.

By making a purchase from Guideposts, you join our community in touching millions of lives, inspiring them to believe that all things are possible through faith, hope, and prayer. Your continued support allows us to provide uplifting resources to those in need. Whether through our communities, websites, apps, or publications, we inspire our audiences, bring them together, and comfort, uplift, entertain, and guide them. Visit us at guideposts.org to learn more.

We would love to hear from you. Write us at Guideposts, P.O. Box 5815, Harlan, Iowa 51593 or call us at (800) 932-2145. Did you love *Star of Wonder: Dobah's Story*? Leave a review for this product on guideposts.org/shop. Your feedback helps others in our community find relevant products.

Find inspiration, find faith, find Guideposts.
Shop our best sellers and favorites at
guideposts.org/shop
Or scan the QR code to go directly to our Shop

More Great Mysteries Are Waiting for Readers Like *You*!

Whistle Stop Café

"Memories of a lifetime...I loved reading this story. Could not put the book down...." —ROSE H.

Mystery and WWII historical fiction fans will love these intriguing novels where two close friends piece together clues to solve mysteries past and present. Set in the real town of Dennison, Ohio, at a historic train depot where many soldiers set off for war, these stories are filled with faithful, relatable characters you'll love spending time with.

Extraordinary Women of the Bible

"This entire series is a wonderful read.... Gives you a better understanding of the Bible." —SHARON A.

Now, in these riveting stories, you can get to know the most extraordinary women of the Bible, from Rahab and Esther to Bathsheba, Ruth, and more. Each book perfectly combines biblical facts with imaginative storylines to bring these women to vivid life and lets you witness their roles in God's great plan. These stories reveal how we can find the courage and faith needed today to face life's trials and put our trust in God just as they did.

Secrets of Grandma's Attic

"I'm hooked from beginning to end. I love how faith, hope, and prayer are included...[and] the scripture references... in the book at the appropriate time each character needs help. —JACQUELINE

Take a refreshing step back in time to the real-life town of Canton, Missouri, to the late Pearl Allen's home. Hours of page-turning intrigue unfold as her granddaughters uncover family secrets and treasures in their grandma's attic. You'll love seeing how faith has helped shape Pearl's family for generations.

Learn More & Shop These Exciting Mysteries, Biblical Stories & Other Uplifting Fiction at **guideposts.org/fiction**